POEMS AND OTHER FAIRY TALES 1968–2020

POEMS
and OTHER FAIRY TALES
1968–2020

Kees Nydam

Can you keep a secret? In 1962, I was 8 turning 9 and Malvina Reynolds penned a chart busting satirical song called 'Little Boxes'. She wrote about pretty children going to summer camp and then on to university. Some would become lawyers, and of these lawyers, some would go into copyright law. In turn these folk would generate ISBNs to put into boxes, like the one below. In a parallel universe, exists a narrative of song-catchers who channel the songs of the village community, each a 'medium' who captures what is already there. Thus, ownership of these songs belongs to the whole. The same could be said about poetry. Using a basic mental model, stealing from one is plagiarism, thieving from thousands is research. Mark Twain, recognising this conundrum, said "Only one thing is impossible for God: To find any sense in any copyright law on the planet." My secret is that my inner 8 or 9 year-old child thinks that copyright law, is very *ticky-tacky*. Only those familiar with the song will get the reference! Awkward then, that in order to nurture our inner children, the grown-ups in the global village need to earn a crust. D'oh!

I am comforted though that no one reads anything written on the copyright page. So, this secret is safe. At least I hope so.

✔

First published in 2021 by Echo Books
an imprint of Superscript Publishing Pty Ltd
ABN 76 644 812 395
Suite 401, 140 Bourke St, Melbourne VIC 3000
www.echobooks.com.au

ISBN: 9781-1-922603-00-5

PROLOGUE

At school, I seriously sucked at spelling and grammar. So, I apologise in advance in case my 'spelling and grammar' make your eyes bleed. In my defence, I railed against what I considered the shambolic rules corralling the written word. In a visceral sense, I was more drawn to the clip-clap of sonics. The crafted harvesting of spoken words could make music. I dug poetry, verse and their sibling, lyrics. I continue to dig them.

I have no right to expect a reading audience, as I have not really suffered for my 'art'. I'm thus not entitled. I would chide being viewed as a tortured poet as my *torturer*s were a troupe of beneficent life-coaches. Each work denotes a page in my personal 'diary', a piece of abstract word-art painted in and coloured by artistic code that invites deciphering. Equally, each work is lacquered with rhythmic texture and musicality. Ultimately, these poems and fairy tales, helped me to make sense of my rich set of life-experiences.

My hope is that these creations resonate with you, and maybe even cause a pleasurable sense-quake of the spiritual kind. My son, Vincent, has been my much-valued editor and co-developer in many of the works. I have credited him as co-author where his contribution has been significant. We will be thrilled if our musings inspire you to explore your own inner poet.

My attempt to group each work into themes, works but only to a point. Some bridge several themes. The earliest piece was written in 1968 and the latest in 2020. Charley, Abbey and Kate (my two talented daughters) and Bram (a cousin) contributed to the complementary sketches. Carolyn (my wife) carried out the mammoth task of final proof reading.

Please enjoy,

Kees

CONTENTS

LOVE AND INTIMACY

GRATITUDE

INNER CHILD AND OTHER FAIRY TALES

MEDICINE AND SICK-OLOGY

MORALITY, STRUGGLE AND CONFLICT

MORTALITY AND IMMORTALITY

MY CHILDREN

ART, MUSIC
and MOVEMENT

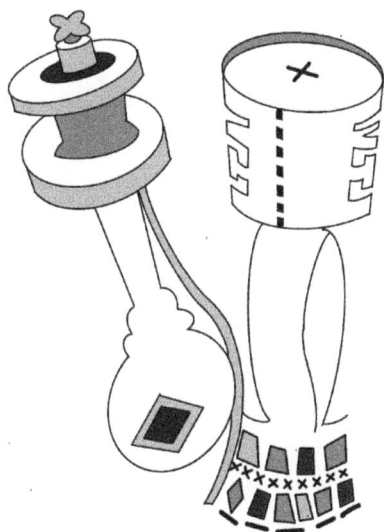

Chess Wheels Keep on Turning

FAIRGROUND

Wonder if...
Do notice
Consider...
Copy that
Go figure
Drums-a-heartbeat
Stop d**king around

▲

Ideas
All suss
Monkey d**ks
Abound
Bars belief
White noise-a-din
Stop d**king around

▲

Grace
Who needs it
Zip here
Lickety split
Karma's barred
Its light is loud
Stop d**king around

▲

So, who's
Joining in
To this circuit
Luck-a-round
Who'll benefit
From this Fairground
Stop d**king around

▲

Let's look | Above the noise
The eye is where | atop the din
It sees true | The truth is
Plain child play's | Raucous
Reining on a carousel | It's SOS hurls thin
Well after youth | I state again
Stop d**king around | Stop d**king around

▲ ▲

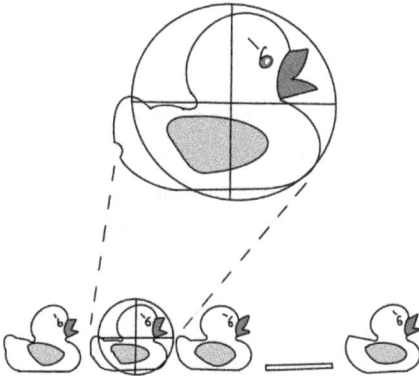

There-is-no-situation-right-now
There-is-no-stimulation-some-how
This-is-no-simulation-of-TAO
*There-is-no-situation-right-now**

Open Season @ the Fairground

'The key to happiness is letting each situation be what it is instead of what you think it should be' – Mandy Hale

DO-DO-DO DERVISH

Whirling, howling
The 'BEING' in trance
A body in prayer
A prayer called dance

◆

A rapturous life
Of craze and wonder
Flammable magic
Open to chance

◆

Beaming a light on
The fervour of heart
A bridge to the truth
Over tranquil lakes

◆

Do-do surrender
Do try to avoid
Getting down on yourself
Go make some mistakes

Life without music
Would be a mistake
Cause a life without music
Might just see you break

◆

Each spin, draws in – as well as out
A heart, on fire – gives up, many secrets
The more, you let in – the more, you'll receive
Ignore laws of logic – discount everything
Do-do-do Dervish
Do-do-do Dervish

◆

Go fly with wings
Made from mind and grace
Know it all ends
Back where it begins

◆

Body committed
But the soul stays still
Don't need wings to fly
Just simply the will
Don't waste your time
On far flung dimensions
Spin like a top
Caught in an abyss

◆

Decline to squander
Degrees of freedom
Don't waste the chance
Of true happiness

Each spin, draws in – as well, draws out
A heart, on fire – gives up, many secrets
The more, you let in – the more, you'll receive
Reject your own logic – let all, fill within
Do-do-do Dervish
Do-do-do Dervish
Do-do-do Dervish
Do-do-do Dervish

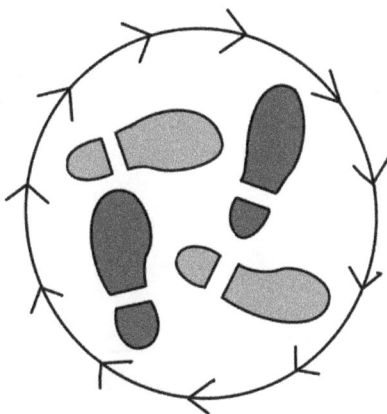

Dance Instructions For One

'That is happiness; to be dissolved into something complete and great' - Willa Cather, novelist (1873-1947)

Bargara   Dec 2018

MONET'S GARDEN

Born to impress
Hungry for raw originalness
He caught his own retinal sense
Locking a reverent resonance

He was to start a displaced gent
Brushing about a misplaced town
Until his chanced colours
Found a place of their own

His palate secured
Crisp colours to sight
The garden-fresh slant
Brisk tints at their best

Courting scrutiny
A shimmering banter
Conformity's great
Non-conformity's better

Canons kept
Standards sacked
He promised to detonate
Till spent and his body surrendered

Jade green shutters
How audacious is that?
Do they invite the garden in?
Or draw the insides out?

Either way
I tilt my panama hat
To a hallowed anthophile
A sacred one at that

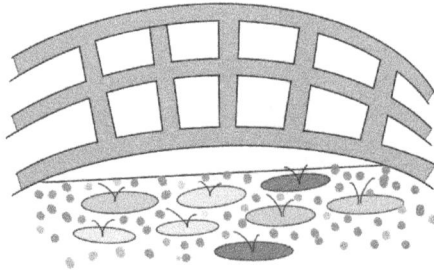

Foot Bridge over Lily Pond in Monet's Garden

Giverny, France   August 2016

16

GO

Hoick-one-two, Roger that
Yank em up, stomachs flat
Show pride, flaunt piazzas
Sock it to 'em, n' all that jazz
Go

This just in, but in too deep
Escape plan, bracket creep
Pick a line, make it through
Big move, road trip
Go

Comfort zones, fine and all
Only there no magic happens
Break down a door, be a Wild Card
Leave 'em always wanting more
Go

Be willing to own ya crazy
own ya messy

You want magic, just look 'round you
Make yourself savvy, see what's clearly
true
They tried to ditch the witch
But the who, the what, the why
Did never die

We all curate our outer self
To best cite us
Anything to get us to
A special cave in Kathmandu

When our journeys collide
Just be sure they coincide
With the inner self's purpose
That will in the end not hurt us

If you say you want to be alone
Then don't complain that you are lonely
It's the sad ones who arrive on their own
At the end of the journey

Go – Bram Ket

In Naples, traffic lights are merely a suggestion

Brisbane   Nov 2019

GHOST @ TOP TABLE

Ali lived to be a writer
Made a play of folding words
Plying rhymes to make 'em sweeter
Then hand 'em on to troubadours
Ali's wants were somewhat humble
Not for him the frontman's fame
Just a ghost @ the top table
Anonymity his game

✖

His words were magic; they promised Shangri-la
Mere conjured dreams; boding utopia

The glory sought, just in-the-knowing
His fertile notes freed to inspire
No need for handprints on the *Boulevard*
Just a gilt-edged pen-4-hire
Keeping clear of validation
Absent from curtain calls
His entrusted "star-harlequins"
Were more equipped and on the ball

✖

His words were magic, they promised Shangri-la
Mere conjured dreams, heartbeat utopia

Ghost at the table; nothing's as it seems
Ghost at the table; they conjured dreams
Ghost at the table; nothing's as it seems
Ghost at table; conjuring dreams

✖

At best ethereal, driven home on just a wink
They conjured dreams, hearts beat-in-sync
At best ethereal, driven home on just a wink
They conjured dreams, hearts beat-in-sync

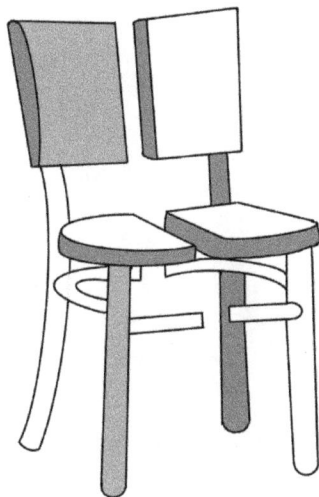

Vincent's Chair

9-Miles-High//Brisbane-Budapest-via Dubai   2018

HAIKU REFUGEES

Haiku conversations
Words with care cue
Netting certain meaning
'Bout what, who knew

Light legato whispers
Volleying vowels that thread
Elbowing out consonants
And what it was we said

My bad, I got the question right
Bar the tone, which was amiss
So sad, you then got the answer wrong
Back and forth we duelled all night
Till finally we kissed

Your bearing looms in disguise
Your mask designed to feign
Underneath-the-radar man
At 6 o'clock we'll try again

Our goal as refugees
Decked in ancestral dress
It's not so much, as so bare
Basic nonetheless
White noise, we Haiku Refugees

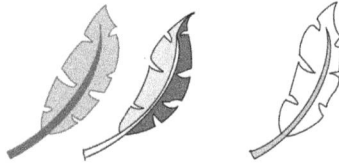

We Are Just A Feather on God's Breath

Ah yes, language... such a blunt instrument!

K&V Nydam   Bargara   Sept 2018

RAIN DANCE

Cyclone breaks, so where you gonna go
Heaven shakes, dial-in radio
Don't hide away and wait its pass
You're better than that, you've got class
Do a rain dance

Cloudbursts surge, what you gonna do
Torrents fall, cue-in a soft-shoe
Do a rain dance, Do a rain dance

Oye – yes you "Twinkle Toes"
House, hip-hop, workout them shoes
Freestyle, you get to choose
Do a rain dance

So, the dancers shine
Such a flair display
Is the talent only theirs?
Or is the hurricane
A tutor hid in plain sight

Rain Dance

'Life isn't about waiting for the storm to pass;
it's about learning to dance in the rain' - Vivian Greene

Bundaberg   2015-2018

SPARKLING WANGST

COG FOG hits my brain
As I down my next drink
How on earth do I remain here
And not overshoot or under-think

Titration's oh-so-tricky
And I'm trying oh-so-hard
Not to trip on shards-o-glass
That catches me off guard

What do you think-n'-all?
Hapless, only when straight
There are events in our lives
That are quite disparate

It's only existential
If it comes from France
Otherwise, it's just sparkling wangst
Which gives you half a chance

She yanked me anchor
Wit' zero compassion
Cut a hole in my soul
Like it was in fashion

Served anyway-u-like
Run smooth or rough
Too much fun
Is never quite enough

What have we done?
And is it our fault?
What of the consequence
D+M… sparkling wangst

Cog Fog

K&V Nydam   Valencia, Spain   Oct 2019

STRAW-MAN

Paint me a picture
Use lots of colour
In sections with numbers
Don't cross the borders

Tell me a story
Make it a sweet one
Apply lots of lust
Add love if you must

Play me a ditty
Make it sound pretty
Roll out the baseline
Cast chills down my spine

Mister Strawman
He does this because he can

Write me a play
About spoils in the hay
Make me a strawman
Part of your game plan

Build me a dream
Ever a wet one
Where all bets are off
For getting it on

Concoct me a potion
Mix in some emotion
Make it taste richer
Paint me a picture

Sister Strawman
She does this because she can

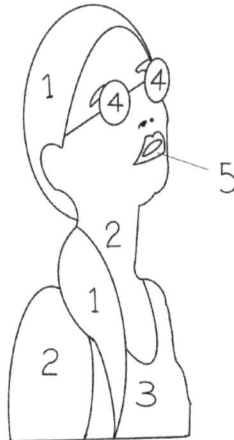

Paint By Numbers

Mon Repos & Bargara   2010 -2018

THE DANCER

What of this to me
And what would it have me feel in the darkness
It is tense and serious, and the weight drives me harder
Throwing forewords my projection

OK, I'll dance for you, you will watch
I will take your full commitment
And I will remain untouched
Protected by the darkness
Protected by the movement
Surrounded by the swirl of the Dancer

One of these days when they come
to turn on the lights
I may not care to return anymore

Dancer

Menangle   1986

24

THE MOON

I wanna be nimble n' scrappy
An' make folk happy
As if we were juveniles again
I wanna be the rising tide
Uplifting all those by my side
Leaving a wake of smiles, that's the plan

A man and his deckhand
Were never left astrand
They hitched a ride with the tide
In step and side-by-side
With mindful harmony, back once more
In their stride, where they'd been before

There'll be no mindless drinking here
We're all drinking with purpose
Hoping to get there soon
Our mission, time critical
We must be analytical
Travelling by the light of the Moon

There's always some
Fact in the surreal
A new angle or tack for a deal
There's always more
That's for sure
Light to travel and then some

You say you exist
So how do I respond
I am the universe, remember
You might shudder, but I won't quake
I am totally awake to you
I am the fire and you are the ember

I wanna be nimble 'n scrappy
Fully sick an' happy, with irony there
By the light, of the Moon

Galileo's Moon in 1610

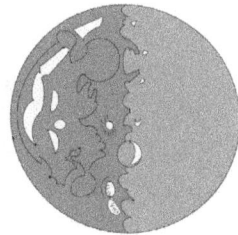

Inspiration: 1. lunch with Di Wills   2. The Waterboys, 'The Whole of The Moon' (1985)

K&V Nydam   Bargara   Nov 2019

ULTRA-NU WAY – TUMBLEWEED

Confluence, everywhere
Even in silence,
It lingers there

There's force and energy in pairing
For welding
Needs heat

Creation takes ruin
Without loss
No one wins

Collect select
N' brew the new
Tumbleweed begets tumbleweed

Be advised by the bias
When talking
Begins

Confluence influence
The union
Of things

New versions, old versions
Perversions
Hold sway

Mashup: time warp
Wake up to
The next new day

The circle begins
Never ends
In an ultra-new way

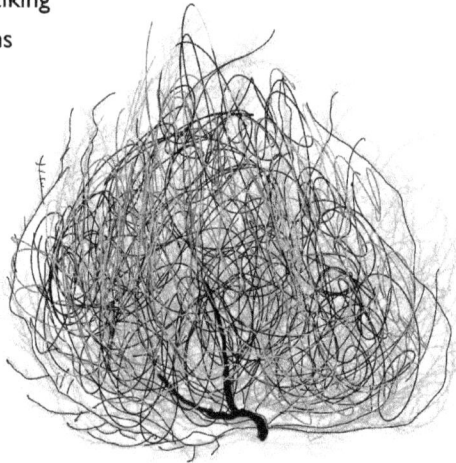

Tumbleweed Yarn

Bargara   Dec 2019

VINCENT VAN G

There's the problem
S'all bunk
With jillions eager
Who'd-a-thunk
Handfuls-o-vison
Kept us spellbound
Yet peering beneath
Here's what we found

History is meant
For those who don't care
For what's real...
Artists beware
Cut the cards
And just deal...

All those words
That exit your mouth
Bare bone history
Gone south
So, you cut off
Your bothersome ear
What were you thinking
What did you fear

A suicide yarn
Based on false pretence
Bad history, worse psyche
René's bare defence
A joke, dodgy gun
Just bad "fate"
O' Really, come on... mate

The kid's dodgy gun
Did the job real well
When Moira was consorted
The barrel coughed and by destiny's
will
It did go off the day it shot
Vincent van Gogh

What Did You Say?

Reference: Gregory White Smith & Steven Naifeh,
'NCIS: Provence: The Van Gogh Mystery', *Vanity Fair*, 7 November 2014
https://www.vanityfair.com/culture/2014/12/vincent-van-gogh-murder-mystery

K&V Nydam   Brisbane   Feb 2019

AUSTRALIANA

Beds are Burning

ANDY

Move 'm out	Eight kid-pilgrims
Seated in	Reach da border
A desert ship	Voiding space
Kids again	And muting time
Recouping calm	Wading through sands
A moral compass check	Of a once icy sea
Brought back	Till the sun cut it loose
Into line	Forging new sanctuary

On Ochre Mesa, Holy Man makes a Plan

Cloistered from now
Retreating to ever-were
Free-range and eager
Juvie and wild

So far from da water
Not just in distance, but also in
time
Eight kid-pilgrims reach da border
Phasing space and muting time

On Ochre Mesa
Holy Man makes a plan
An' with air of resignation
Calls for private Ramadan

Andy can you help me
I know you got the wherewithal
Fix it, so the motor never starts
Abandoned, we can have it all

Red sand spills
Between our fingers
Like something is there
But then nothing at all

Quitting swags
Inhaling dawn
Chilly gold turns to blue
We take awe in it all

So far from the water
Not just in distance, but also in
time
Fresh life erupts; adapts anew
And this might dazzle
If you see it at all

And it might get loud if you hear it at all

Simpson Desert   Sept 2015

BATTLE ON RICHMOND HILL

diverging minds – too close to matter
high-time to gulp – a dry-spit-pill
cock gun bolt – old cold-eyed killer
eyeing fresh sniper-prey
on Richmond Hill

alluvial rich was the earth where we bleed
the sanctioned age had come
lightning thrash found – and fully thumped me
boggy brain wept – heave hoe
my dark favorite foe

much ado – no coupling manhood
they did their best to bash-burn-bury me
beneath the earth – where we bleed
and none recalled that
I was a seed

Don't Bash-Burn-Bury Me

we understood – each other
not much though – came unstuck long ago
time leave me – out of your life-plans
memories are me
actions are null

■

the nascents called out – in white hot fury
to the 'Black-Hand' boy – if ever there be one
the ancients called back – but much more clearly
"don't do things fast
just do them well"

■

crack! gun-bolt rings – and made the Guardians sing
And oh, my God – I could tell
the Richmond Hill Battle – had but saved me
"don't do things fast
just do them well"

K&V Nydam   Richmond NSW   2017

BETSY BELL*

Why're you here
Your home's the sky
Ms. Pierian Muse
On whom eight did rely
You did as you were asked
Until the dice were cast

Now curio art
Set deep on high
Hiding a truth
Along with a lie
Pablo gave air to that
Move chocks, push contact

Our sorrow's naught
No, nothing at all
Unless it grows something
No matter how small
Who's liberating who
Who's liberating you

Looking grave
In a loft somewhere
Your purpose was to fly
Not lie solitaire
Who's liberating who
Who's liberating you

There're no winners
Here to be seen
Clearly at a glance
War brings brutal things
Like this lady's show and tell
Barely noticed, Betsy Bell

Once your roar
Echoed a pounding drum
That drove a beating heart
Higher and then some
Why the hell, Betsy Bell
Yeah, how come you fell?

* Beautiful Betsy is a Second World War Liberator bomber that crashed in Kroombit Tops National Park
on 26 February 1945, on a flight from Darwin to Brisbane.

Freedom

'Art is a lie that makes us realize the truth' – Pablo Picasso
'Art is not a mirror held up to reality, but a hammer with which to shape it' – Bertolt Brecht

Bargara   2017-19

HiLUX HOMBRES

Toyotas streaming
Convoys of dust
Machismo machines
That never rust
Executive Order
"Build market share"
Collateral damage!
No matter; don't care

No animals harmed
In this ad campaign
Not so for the Hombres
At all times fair game
Executive Order:
"Make Bigger the Brand"
Informal Prayer:
"Play nice in the Sand"

River Crossing

So, comic ironic
The ambiguous mask
The Branding might suffer
Ah – you may well ask

"War – What Is It Good for….
Absolutely Nothing" (APPARENTLY)
So, they sang years ago (*Can't remember when*)
Chiro's people called Abu Bakr
'Bout product placement
Somewhere near

❖

So, comic ironic
The ambiguous mask
The Branding might suffer
Ah – you may well ask

Toyotas streaming… (*on the PLASMA screen*)
Convoys of dust… (*you MOVE me*)
Machismo machines… (*you're so SEXY*)
That never rust… (*in YOU we trust*)
Executive Order… (*IMPERIAL*)
"Build market share" … (*I NEED one*)
Collateral damage… (*SO REASONABLE*)
No matter; don't care… (*I SHOULD think so*)

Simpson Desert   September 2016

INFINITY HORIZON

From a nearby waterway
Yellow-ketchup lilies waved
Dust devils curled up the track
Dispatched by a bullock-dray

We stared down a masterclass
Gravel mōrēs for living
There before a shadow wall
In private and in common

Touting out from the edge
They trespassed and some would fall
We gave praise to pioneers
With sure kudos, action verbs an' all

Unperturbed at times austere
And ravished by the fading sun
We felt their elder's souls within
Their writings made that crystal clear

Ambitious to make it count
They had the grit of sheer granite
To be the pray of raptors
'Tis hard to know which pinch of straw
Would be the rogue that made them fall
And so, transform to crazed captors
They had each other's back
And safeguarded one another's soul

Past present and yet to come
Let us toast the immigrants
Trekking the Savanna Gulf
Who relish quest and then some

From Cairns to Mataranka
With Adels Grove along the way

Infinity

Dedicated to Ludwig Leichhardt, Ludwig Moonie, Ludwig Fletcher & Co.
'Moonlight – Electric Cello (Inspired by Beethoven)' – The Piano Guys
https://www.youtube.com/watch?v=DRVvFYppUOw

Savannah Way Nth Qld   April 2019

ULURU
[A DIFFERENT REIGN]

Dawn bares many things
All pure, real and reasonable
Crispy-calm, clear and chicane
A windfall woman; another miracle

Taboo, but ever paramount
Tell me who wrote this account:
Here nature paints, the next dot
Were da Vinci just could not

Time shifts, hearts stand down
Day is done and leisure's come
Under stars, a brash tribute
Recalls a tomb that we salute

Now two tribes, commence to feast
Fired by She-Lizard's dance
Buoyed, emboldened and in a trance
Revving riling, ire and chance

Angry hosts, inciting wrath
Mud sculptures, start to roust
Ancestors rumble, spacetime collides
Crossing where, two serpents joust

Haunting clicks of message sticks
Just added to the call
Uluru weeps to another rain
Standing steady, valiant and tall

Totems fall amidst the storm
Leaving two with blood on hand
They alone assigned to rule
Sacred Serpents of the sand

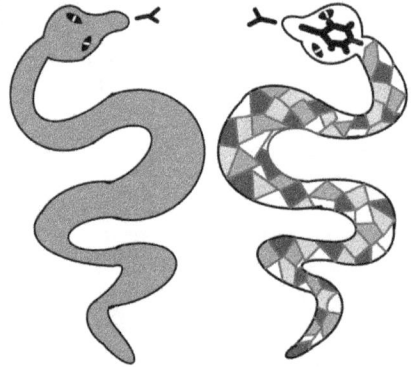

Uluru Serpents

Soundtrack: Carl Weingarten, *A Different Rain*

Uluru   July 2017

MAYDAY–MAYDAY
[KINTSUKUROI – 1]

Wildfire mayday, mayday wildlife
Venez m'aider, da-suffocating passion
You cried slow, but did it so fast
Hoping for more dynamite ration

Spitball away, here come da-joker
Fame's hazardous, fa-dose de-mediocre
Bid us recall, a contradiction
Life's consequence of this hazard-addiction

Mayday wildlife, I'm going down
Blow cover, break glass, eject...
Cry slow, but do so fast
Hoping to make the jùjú last

Love-ladies bubble in the bain-marie
Cœur de pirate, kept warm and waiting for me
Quell core spirit, what's that to be
Ablaze in ways, an' served up in life's-ghee

Dark silken girls wave granted permission
Their smile is worth da price for admission
Falling glacial in motion is compellingly rife
Pleasure's is there, fixing broke cups-of-life

K&V Nydam   Savannah Way, Nth Qld   May 2019

MAYDAY–MAYDAY
[KINTSUKUROI – 2]

Wildfire mayday, mayday wildlife
Venez m'aider, da-suffocating passion
You cried slow, but did it so fast
Hoping to stretch da-holy-dynamite ration

Spitball away, here come da-joker
Fame's hazardous, fa-dose de-mediocre

Mayday wildlife, I'm going down
Blow cover, break glass, eject – I hit one
You cried slow, but did so fast
Hoping to make da-dynamite remain some

Love-ladies bubble in the bain-marie
Cœur de pirate, kept warm and waiting for me
Quell core spirit, what's that to be
Ablaze in ways, an' served up in life's-ghee

Bid us recall, a contradiction
Life's consequence of this hazard-addiction

Mayday wildlife, I'm going down
Blow cover, break glass, eject – I hit one
You cried slow, but did it fast
Hoping to make da-dynamite last

Dark silken girls wave granted permission
Their smile is worth da price for admission
Falling glacial in motion is compellingly rife
Pleasure's is there, fixing broke cups-of-life

Lights come on, each Friday night
Throw down the cloak, play at fever pitch
Waking up to a world, that haunts you
Wanton stole time, detached and now out of reach

Leaking oil and stalling for time
Wanting, hoping, t' fix the cup-o-life

Memory hobbles, the march of time
Rebukes the past attempts at fidelity
Real is a place, for da-unknown face
Memory is a land of treachery

Mayday wildlife, I'm going down
Blow cover, break glass, eject – I hit one
You cried slow, but did so fast
To da-dynamite, hoping not to succumb

If the threads of "now"
crossed us at a speed
faster than light,
would we have seen
what happened last night.
Would it have even
happened at all

Last Night

K&V Nydam   Auckland NZ   May 2019

EUROPEAN HISTORY
and THE CLASSICS

Forest – Kate Gould

HAIL COLUMBUS

Gusts of glory blew Columbus
Hell-bent on sailing into the mist
But for grubstake, ever canny
He lured Bella into his tryst

As part showman; more part liar
Flaunting his vainglory claim
Awash with myth; this Genoese trier
Fame and wealth was his endgame

Cristoforo – more arse than class
Never short of self-belief
He placed his faith in adventure
With a side-order of mischief

Raise a toast to Columbus
Toady to Queen Isabella
He held a venal moral compass
And was a kinda complex fella

Hail Columbus – we salute you
For all the risks that you ran
Your navigation was amazing
But you failed as a man

All in Isabela's Name

K&V Nydam   Melbourne   2020

KING ARTHUR & SIR LANCELOT

From high hopes to high-end
And with noble regret
Art held his place
Rightly left of centre-staged

Parleying with friends
Part shaded by dusk
Clinking cups and mugs
Smug and blood bathed

The fabled King forged
From Wōden's Norsemen
Art led his gang
Of Demon Horsemen

Clothed in courage
Dashing mid-mist
Ethos stark – pathos plain
With logic hard to resist

Excalibur gave
Sharp logic à la sword
The Saxons did yield
To Art, their new Lord

For armed conquest
Was Art's fond whore
T'was war he adored
Thus, forsaking his Queen

Abandoned at home
Gwenevere did begin
To have her soul search
For a new love to win

In the right eye
And well persuaded
Sir Lancelot traded
His King for Gwen

Two-edged Crown

'Maybe all one can do is hope to end up with the right regrets' – Arthur Miller (1915–2005)

K&V Nydam   Bundaberg   2018

CHARLEMAGNE

From coy nymph to noble bride
Pantomiming the butterfly
Silk-adorned, her sculpture shone
Climbin' t'ward the throne

"Back yourself" her mater urged
When Woden rings the bell
Roland – that Great Paladin
Yes, even his sword fell

Laconic sire, staid and endowed
Mans the sideline orchestrating
When pressed, "because" will suffice
Cajole your blue-blood valentines

What happens next is in your hands
Make sure no one sees it coming
There is power in serenity
The sorcerers are humming

The priestess spoke "Damn the vain"
In the Court of Charlemagne
The Franks were dead-on wonderful
For men did or did they reign

Men aren't rulers long; their lives are over quick
The man-foe is obvious; their numbers soon deplete
Raised to colonise; the damsel-play's more slick
Disguised as fragile butterflies, keen withal discrete

■

From coy nymph to noble bride
Pantomiming a butterfly
Silk-adorned, her sculptures shone
She commandeers the throne

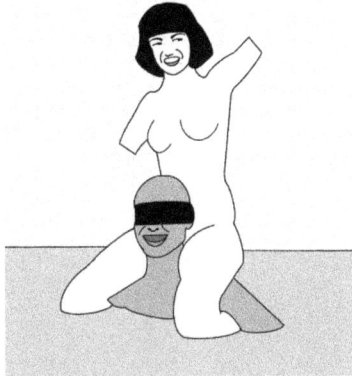

Water Nymphs Rule

'Man is certainly stark mad; he cannot make a worm, and yet he will be making gods by dozens' – Michel de Montaigne.

TRAVEL and EXPLORATION

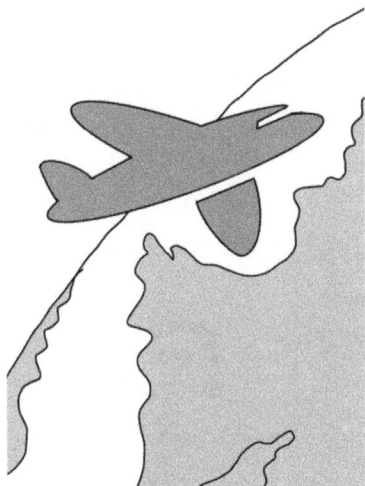

GULF OF OMAN

Blind to time
I recall
SOMETHING that maybe
never happened at all

Our need to trust
in HIGHER LORE
was so much more
than our want to rule

Then near Oman
KHAN put me straight
"command the horse
then master man's fate"

Opaque to place
I MARKED a space
between Father Sky
and Mother Earth

Aroused and assured
to irk strife
I broke a mare
then took a WIFE

There, I seized the need to keep
the black powder dry
so, our SCIONS could for good
ignite their own spark to fly

Our hunger for
common flesh
was HUNGER
for a God

If in
a LABYRINTH lies life
without fear of birth
then why on earth
should I fear to die

Born free
and ever wild
she bucked all night
we BORE a child

10,000 Maniacs

'As I have not worried to be born, I do not worry to die' – Federico García Lorca (1898-1936)

Bundaberg   Nov 2018

HAWK-EYE

Satori moment on the precipice
Do I fly or just fall
Don't step back – play the endgame
So much the better – be enthralled

●

Cannot linger for a longish while
The era's ending – time to tack
No wonder – put all doubt on ice
The instant is now; won't be stonewalled

●

Eggshell smarts from the get-go
The past – a rut – turned sour
Memory loaded to the brim by man
'Cept nix of value – solely sham

●

There's welcome cheer in forgetting
Focus annuls all
Brings back game and gains up purpose
Pumping air beneath my wings

There is – for some – a counterplay
Flight or fall – a conjoint thrill
I ache to see via the peregrine's eye
In his stuka-dash to kill

●

There's grace in carnal excess
Abandon's the key to wake
I hurt for the rush of
The next-to-last mistake

●

The Hawk's my soul to the abyss
How he moves sheer genius
I will be one among them
There is truth in their genus – Amen

Hawkeye

Channel Nigel Kennedy, punk violinist

Bargara   2017

53

JUST READ THE BLOODY SIGNS

Got into a spot of bother
Held hostage by technology
Castaway sans Google map
The roaming thing, a phony

●

I glided into Singapore
Before my techs could flick the switch
Mein Handy's chip blocked on entry
All web-assist was ditched
Got cold, got wet,
Rain wrecked my hat
Moods fouled, and the rib and I,
Had a spat
But I knew I shouldn't've been like that

●

Due notice to
My need for a handmaiden ICT
I drew notice to
My bonehead need for handheld ICT

Brainstorm and thunder
In my head
My inner worrier
Second-guessing their worth
Gave up trying to be smart
Oh no! Try this. Move on. Try that!
BOOM

Blitzed by a brain wave
It's a frigging vill after all
Just ask a talking human
Dang, what a good call
And if that should stall,
Go read the signs
Due notice to my handmaiden's
Need for ICT
Just read the bloody signs

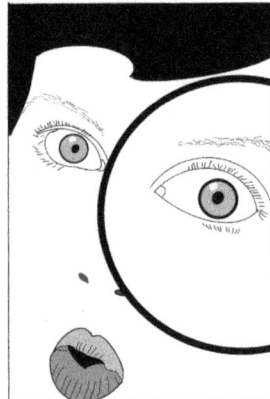

Eyeglass

Channel P!nk 'Waiting for Love'

K&V Nydam   Singapore   August 2016

SHINKANSEN

Renown some – for the umpteenth time
Mad to find – what we'd become
And where – to fix our mind

■

Meanwhile saw us – in a dewy way
A bit less coy – we're joyed to say
An' hell more – wired to play

■

Our touchstone – a green-light zone
That means we go – show 'em we came
More the same – ain't real again

■

Press to the floor
Then down some more
At no point heed
Just give me speed
We'll race the Silver Bullet

■

Blast-off came
Fired off a wink
Wheels turn revolver
With cups in their holder
We skate on a steal ice rink

■

We'll do akin – as birds trust wings
In lieu – branches on trees
We'll bet our trust on all new things

■

Red Sun – Fast Trains
"New Freaks" – Two Lanes
Crazy Fast
We'll bet our trust on all new things

Kyoto-Tokyo Bullet Train   September 2018

LOVE and INTIMACY

Delia

ADVOCATE'S VANGUARD

Riding home at night, in the wet
I was leaving a girl, I had just met
Guess you could say, there was no regret
Riding home in the rain

Wildflowers bloom, down by the creek
Roses smell real fine, in my neighbour's backyard
And if you're wondering, how I pay my bills
I'm Jack, the advocate's vanguard

Do you think I look funny, from where you stand?
My alibi's airtight, my defence stands
It's OK to be curious, OK to just be
Cause I'm just a mirror, and it's yourself that you see

Riding home at night, in the wet
I was just leaving a girl, I had just met
Guess you could say, there was some regret
Riding home in the rain

Wet

Menangle   Mid-1980s

AFTER LOVE

it's after love, when the turning tides at rest,
then is the act of love truly blessed

it's after love
and that last returning tide
that's when is the real caress;

to drift on light laying
with sanctum flesh
without awkwardness;

endeared, in cold wet embrace
now still; lips oval
and half-smiling face

the coition ended
the ego and the id mended
the needs for now, suspended

Dress 2 Impress

Hunters Hill, Sydney   1968

59

BRAND-NEW MISS

Goddam, Goddam
It's my brain, again
Goddam, Goddam
It's my brain, again

✳

The devil in me's dead and gone
T'was never my mind to compete
But you presented such an attraction
I felt I had to...
Meet... it

Chorus

Seems it's come to this
In a situation
Found me a *Brand-New Miss*
Better than the one I...
Came in

Chorus

Now, guess it's come to this
We're all mere debris!
With the "victory" consummated
Was it you who won, or was...
It me

Chorus x 2

✳

Thought I'd say it straight
Just the way it is
You reap only what you sow
So, sow what you wanna reap...
Gee whiz

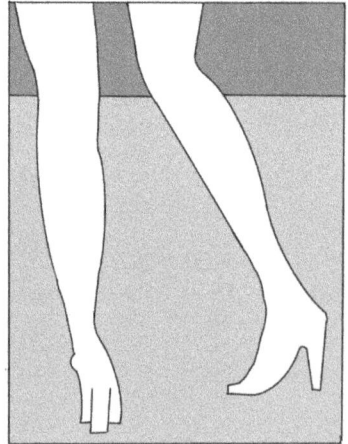

Brand-New Miss

Crow's Nest to Bargara   1970-2018

CAMUS'S GIRL

"Pity the girl at callow sixteen
(Smooth) *in the press of rapt companions*
She bruits her smatter, her bed-lore brag
...prattles the lip-learned light-love list
In (a) *new itch and squirm of sex*
(But)   *how can she foresee?"*
And does it really matter??

By the way...   this time
The dreams are on me
I'll supply the shoulder to cry on
What's her name?   insomnia asks you
Do what you never thought you'd do
Let me see how well you move
To break the ice

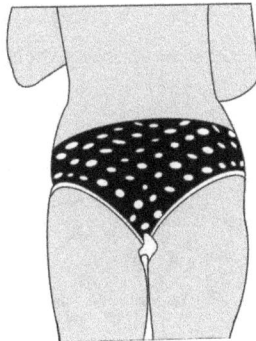

Camus's Girl

Ref: The Stranger from the Dominican monk   Brother Antoninus nee
William Everson, *The Residual Years: Poems, 1934–1948*

Coogee, Sydney   1973

CHEERS 2 TYCHE

was just thinking and I thought
I ought to tell you
that I love you something so bad

Tyche is my favourite name
and dealing dice my favourite game
shoot to win and whip while throwing snake eyes

stay you, stay sweet
stay with me, play it on repeat

dear Lady Luck
my favourite name is YOU
your fruit made me game to fly
you're still the same but now I see
through another's eyes

I love you now and how so bad
I'm at a loss for what to say
stay you, stay sweet
stay the wind upon my sheet

Lady Luck

K&V Nydam   Old Toongabbie   1983

DELIA

WOOD were a campfire site
Now, when begins the night
Everything's alright
Delia, I love ya

WOULD were a potato peel
Now with my Irish blight
Nee can you do me no right
And fetta it gone forever

CAUGHT a word just-ta-day
Blew my swagger clear away
Swayed in with my prance persona
Thought I'd spread my shit round
And FETTA it gone forever

THOUGHT I'd nudge my mien finder
He's not FUNK life willing
Tapped him gently on the shoulder
And he said "find someone else
Go play hide and seek"

CLEARLY quick to the task
Life's hyped-up with days like this
Just a word well hung in space
And FETTA it gone forever

Menangle to Mon Repos   1971-2010

FRAU LUCIFER

Senses wink – primed to kiss
Femme Fatale – a perfect fit
Like cozy warm – hostile once
Danger – for the hell of it

❀

Bait and switch – Miss Lucifer
Who asked you to supper
When tasting wine – gulp, don't spit
Go bareback ride your lover

❀

Now rolling numb – somewhat coy
Born to lead – be followed
Stay calm – through whiplash times
When said and done – we swallowed

❀

Phat bracelets of rhythmic tones
Sound jewelers – forged a score
Mass half-truths – conduct a lie
Cause silence – hurts us more

All I have is now – all I need is you
All I want is love – will you love me too
All I know is what – cannot work out why
Is it any wonder we try to kiss the sky

❀

A canny eye – might gladly try
To heed – as fate draws flack
So, tell me who – gets the better show
Us watching God – Her watching back

❀

Beast untamed – still kind of free
Slam dunk luck – put us there
A Judas Kiss – remembered this
It was never 'bout me

❀

All I have is now – all I need is you
All I want is love – will you love me too
All I know is what – cannot work out why
Is it any wonder we try to kiss the sky

Frau Lucifer

'Excuse me while I kiss the sky' – Jimi Hendrix 1967

Bargara   Feb 2018

JEZEBEL

Jezebel called
From out of the blue
With shameless intent
A trace of treachery too
But who called "time"
To choke each breath of mine

❖

Infamy calls
Dumped in it again
Fireball in the chest
Repeated distain
But what's there to gain
Why go back there again

❖

Jezebel came
Concealed as a sleuth
Dropped fictional cues
Manufacturing truth
But who called "time"
Garrotting each breath of mine
And what's there to gain
Who wants to go back there again

Sure, welcome in
To my home in the zoo
Wearing a grin
Reflector stripes too
But what's there to gain
Who wants to go back there again

❖

Sure, nice cologne
Sweet smell of distain
I've smelt it before
I know why you came
What could I do
My resolve dissolves with you

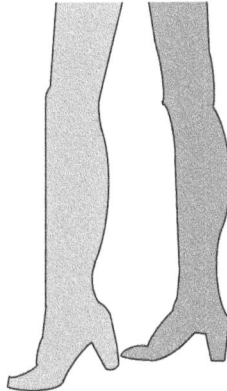

Legs

Mon Repos   2005

MADALENA

She coasted like a galleon
Leaving all else in her wake
A Portuguese man o' war
Armed for arms sake

●

Imposing in full sail
A standard in paragon
Dangerous for certain
Auditioning a c'mon

●

I want a night that never ends
I want time that bends
Into a circle and stretches
And never makes amends

She was a heart-time bandit
And I so gladly gave
She warmed my brain from outside in
Her soul became my cave

●

Her venom intoxicated
With the taste of the sea
Her tentacles a tight embrace
That crushed my breath from me

●

Pixies - 'Magdalena'

Madrid   June 2019

66

MATIE'S SONG

Changes make me happy
Like a moving herd of beasts
People make it all worthwhile
Curious at least
Flocks of white cockatoos
Circling yonder tree
I will sing a song for you
Then you'll sing a song for me

Well it's all right
Sitting on my balcony
I will sing a song for you
You'll sing a song for me

Take me forewords
Take me back
Sometimes I get lost
Along that lonesome track
Time means changes
That all seem worthwhile
You will make me happy
I will make you smile

Chorus

Sometimes I need silence
Wine glass in hand
Green fields roll before my door
Mother Nature's land
Picking away a favourite tune
On my old guitar
Finally, when the sun goes down
We'll be looking up at the stars

Well it's all right
Sitting on my balcony
I will sing a song for you
You'll sing a song for me

Cockatoos

Menangle   1988

MAYBE

Maybe I've forgotten OR
Maybe, I don't want to know
Talking to the bottle
Cause it don't mind
Maybe I've forgotten exactly
How to tell past from future
Just take another sip
And unwind

I've been there
And I've done that
And it's only until morning
And you see the sun rise

●

Found a little trouble
Finally caught with a man
Can't give him respect
Only sorrow
I've got some fine wine
And the night's a little cold
Wine takes care of your sorrow
I'll stay here for you to hold

●

Chorus

Could be there's a scheme
Could be there's a plot
Maybe there are dots to join
Maybe there's not
The story's unfolding
The credits are rolling out
Sunrise lights up the way
Helps you stay the route

●

Chorus

Fruit of the Vine

Menangle   1988

68

MIRROR MEDUSA

Steady – here comes trouble
Don't flinch – get set to run
Stand – outside the huddle
Be ready – to jump the gun

Please – do – be wary
Please – do not – succumb
Things – may get – scary
Or – it could be – fun

Don't engage
In her dead-eye-stare
Gape at her soul
You know – it's there
Regard her guilt
Sight her shame
Get to the point
You're really
Both the same
A mirror

Devour each other
Down to the core
Exhaust yourselves
And then some more

But just
Don't look into her eyes

Fiction forms
And tries to grapple
With a vital dare
To make you stare

No matter how mad it gets for you
It could always be worse for me
It's not about you
Was ne'er about you
So long as you
Just don't look into her eyes

Medusa Mad Hag

in the air between Bundy and Brisbane   August 2019

MICKIE

Watching you hold out
letching like a cur
shadowed from the sun
kind-a-like some stolid lizard
edging under stone

Well, the market was brisk
with all manner of emotion
some being bought, some being sold
but no one really noticed, the lack of true feeling
as we walked in the crowd alone

That heaven place is mad enough now
that heaven place is gunna get yah now

Mickie, you were had
how come you couldn't see
how come now, it don't you feel so funny
you can't shoot down a bird
when it's flying

✖

It's hard when you get to the end
and find that you're both strangers
you call out and all you hear is a silence
that you really can't understand

That heaven place is mad enough now
that heaven place is gunna get yah now

you can't shoot down a bird when it's flying – Bram Ket

Menangle   1989

MISS MYSTIQUE

Don't know why, I can't behave
Can't understand, what makes me Blue
Don't know 'bout you, but I intend
To have a great day; not just pretend

✳

Let me recount a true-blue tale
Bout comic heroes of my day
They were Good; no, they were Great
No Marvellous, Yes Marvellous

✳

I needed Magic, couldn't wait
Could not abide, why this demand
Gave so much panic to some
Like POW

Let me salute you, Miss Mystique
A Gallant Hero – by the way
You were Good; no, you were Great
No marvellous, Yes Marvellous

✳

I paid the price and took a pew
I would defend your value
Go spread the Marvel News
I'll cry Yahoo

✳

Don't know why, I can't behave
Can't grasp why joy me cry!
Go Mystique, pure magic
Thank you

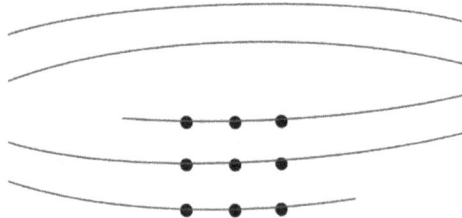

✳

Inside Outside the Box

Inspired by a fortuitous conversation with Yona Harvey (Lady Yoda)

Windmill Café, Bargara   August 2018

NEW WORLD MORALS

Is your cold
Slowly melting
Come to think of it
You'd enjoy the taste
You're holding
Try any need
It leads to where you're longing
If we make it through
Then we make it through

Think of it
As something you always wanted
And if you never had one
Then that's no reason not to try
Something less
Is nothing more than what you're really after
It's just part of the shit
They put in papers
If we make it through
The New World Morals
Then we make it through

Think of it......
As something you always wanted
But when left with it
Which one will you choose?

NWM

Coogee Sydney   1974

SHE-MONARCH AND THE SOLDIER

Her Silence had Power
With which no one messed
Her Cloak, Her Crown
Her Royal Highness

Her Centre-Light a Laser
Detonated from Her Heart
Gentle never, Queen forever
Business always, before pleasure

She stood there breathing
Taking more than air in
Her eyes devouring
His original sin

She had his measure
She'd worked out whether
And plotted when
The hue and cry would begin

He stands now accused
Without knowing why
His discomfort burned
What had he learned
From Her... and now This

The guards duly
Did their duty
So flawlessly
He never knew

There is a soldier
AWOL in a dream
Missing in action
Slayed by Her Laser beam
Her Vivid Light
Straight from Her Heart

Don't mess with the Miss
With the Cloak, the Crown
And the Laser Light
Shot vivid and bright
From Her heart

No slave to common virtue
That is true
Only her need to suppress
Those who knew

No rescue party
For those who mess
With the Chakra Lights
Of the Royal Mistress

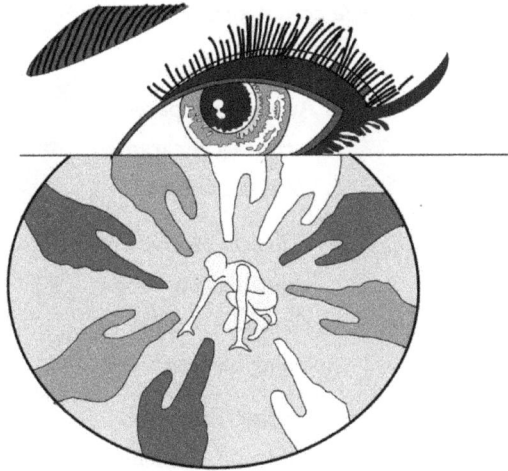

Eye on the Game
[greatly inspired by Shane Foley]

Reference: Suzanna Vega, 'The Queen and the Soldier'

Brisbane   March 2019

TAR ANNE TULA

"Touché-Touché"
I gaily hurled
Spellbound and drawn to
Tula's underworld

"Touché-Touché"
I daren't bow out
She doused my fear
And banished my doubt

"Touché-Touché"
With hooks anchored
Fixed to mate
We commence to conjugate

"Touché-Touché"
At end, I'm spared
Charred fig & caramel
She feasted well

"Touché-Touché"
Appetites at an ebb
Tars was angelic
Spinning her next web

Revived, I survived
This time – *Touché*

Bargara   Jan 2019

WATER-GYPSY
[WANDA]

At birth, you eloped from the sea
Water-gypsies, gave you to me
Love took hold, and pulled me under
By birth, we came to be

You sang, words that made me cry
Blind luck, happenstance and I
Wanton, aimless, too badly alive
To change our minds

With a spur, you bore me back
No more a debtor to my past
Be righteous, nod acknowledgement
The road, in parts, is often bent

Water-Gypsy,
Feeling tipsy
We're both Gypsy
Through and through
And I love you

One soul, behind two blue-kohl eyes
Bonding, laughing, cracking wise
Made me hit on you, 'n then some
By the waves, we turned allies

Concert to another view
Drawn far beyond the pane
Rescue challenged us, 'n then some
Shame held naught to gain

Do you speak Human?
Only in emergency
I'd rather talk Fish
Why — what 'bout you?

Water-Gypsy,
Feeling tipsy
We're both Gypsy
Through and through
And I love you

Wanda

Nielson Park Beach, Bargara   Dec 2018

GRATITUDE

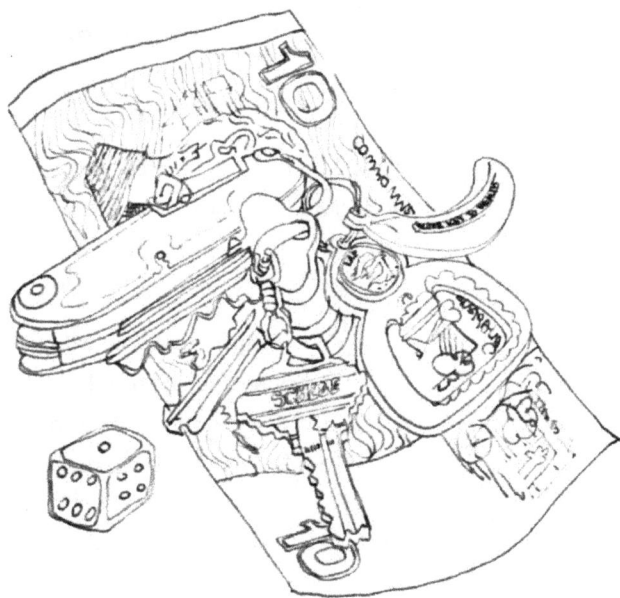

FORK IN THE ROAD

Came upon fork in road
Fine choice to angst about
Caught between diamonds and pearls
Real first-world-matter

Down there, guys in the band
Stare at me guitar in hand
Do we play a quite refrain
Or bash out hardcore operetta

How lucky am I
Stuck with a win-win combo
Lost and ambushed thus
In a can't lose akimbo

Safe and dull... or wild and dangerous
Sound and sheltered... or mad and furious

Brought to boil @ vapour point
Cheery bluff broke overall
Vanished... a fine place to be
Such a neat White Rabbit hole

Uncensored; raw gratitude
Vested in almighty bliss
That which would be so rude
Felicity, my soul's mistress

Down there the guys in the band
Gawk at me guitars in hand
Do we play a quite refrain
Or amp hardcore operetta

How lucky am I
Stuck with this win-win combo
Lost and ambushed thus
Trapped in a can't lose akimbo

Safe and dull... or wild and dangerous;
Sound and sheltered... or mad and furious
Safe and dull... or wild and rapturous;
Good and sheltered... or bad and furious

Life's a game
One-man a-side
A roguish tug-o-war
Played on a mudslide
Always the same
Equal sides
Both strong and tall
All eyes open wide

Down there, guys in the band
Stare at me guitar in hand
Do we play a quite refrain
Or bash out hardcore operetta

Safe and dull... or wild and rapturous;
Good and sheltered... or bad and furious

Brought to boil... at vapour point
Cheery bluff... broke overall
Vanished... a fine place to be
Such a neat... White Rabbit hole

Bargara   2017

GIVING UP WATER

From now I'm a rebel
On the path of subversion
I've taken a vow – I'm giving up water
Because I believe in... insurrection
And not doing what you lot... say I ought-a
So as of today, I'm giving up water

I know I'm a rebel, I am a subversive
Yet I am but fine just the way that I am
I wanna captain my adventure with destiny
And connect with the people and places I love
I wanna live ever-present and accessibly
So as of today, read the above

Hi, I'm a rebel, hear my manifesto
I wanna see all in true focus
I wanna be vulnerable, raw and flawed
I wanna cut the crap and escape the trap
Don't wanna be numb from nothing
So as of today, I'm closing the tap

And because I'm a rebel, I will always want more
I wanna lean t'ward discomfort until its comfortable
I wanna flaunt me fear of disconnection
I wanna be firmer, simpler.... quieter, warmer
Because I believe I'm worthy
And I don't need t' numb nothing
I'm done pretending while I'm huffing and puffing
I wanna let you all know that I'm rough and I'm tough... but still enough
I'm a rebel, I'm giving up water

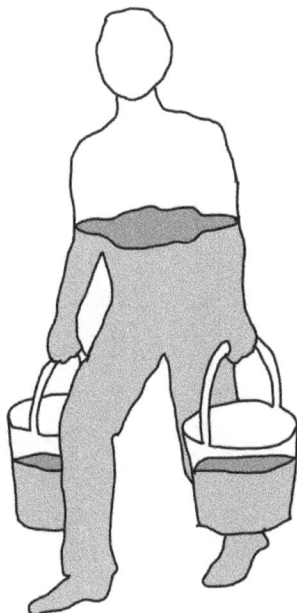

Water Carrying Water Carrier
Carrying Water

'If only I may grow firmer simpler, – quieter, warmer' – Dag Hammarskjöld, *Vägmärken*, 1963

K&V Nydam   August 2020   Bargara

GLAD 2B HERE

have you noticed
how good times
just happen along
and there's no sense
in pursuing the magic

so why go so fast
and see all you see
in a flash
rather, take a slow ride
and savour everything
as you pass

and the feelings
are so calm
the face in the mirror
is less stern and severe
I'm so very glad
to be here
with you all

and I've got a feeling
the good times are starting again
and this time around
they're not gonna end
oh no-no

Coogee Sydney   1972

RETORT-2-[SAMUEL]-BECKETT

Ain't it great to be alive?
"I wouldn't go as far as that"
That "greatness" may be jeopardised
If you over-focus on the fact

As unflinching as it is
The predicament is clear
Life's as precious as it is brief
Until the reaper doth appear

But then life is all we've got
And it sure is a lot
To pay less than your all to it
Is totes a dereliction
So please... do pay attention

Now as the sun
Swarms my skin
I'm doing nothing but hurrying
To slowly take it all in
Come on down
It's great to be living

Floating in life's open sea
The water's touch tickles me
I'm doing nothin' but feelin'
Time stops as I take it all in
Come on down
It's great to be living

Feeling now the giggling breeze
Tiny feathers fan my skin
I'm so alive... yet so at ease
Being still... doing nothing

Ain't it great to be alive?
An understatement that's for sure
Life's allure will ne'er be jeopardised
If you hold your focus on the awe

Fishing Lae (PNG) Style

Reference: Roger Cohen, 'Two deaths and my life', *New York Times International Edition*, 13 January 2020

K&V Nydam   Singapore   Jan 2020

REQUIEM 4A NUN

Requiem 4a Nun* said
"The past is never dead.
It's not even past".
Maybe just in her head
I was never bullied but
I did encounter dicks
Guess I was blessed, a lucky nut
They were just in the mix...
Of it all

●

My formal allocution read
As guilty as I am
Ma moral compass faulted some
T'was all in Faulkner's plan
Drake was just a story
Conjured to address
I guess I was blessed
They were just in the mix...
Of it all

●

MC

86

Early on averted
From toxic consequence
Like the dog that caught the car
I didn't know what's next
I finally slept
Ten hours last night
I was truly blessed
It was just in the mix...
Of it all
We reject sobriety
For it narrows our scope
Through which to view Cauduro's vista
Of camaraderie and hope
In da High Court Mexico
Clearly, I was blessed
It was just in the mix...
Of it all

●

"I know what I've given you
But not what you've received"
Antonio Porchia said that
Who by word or fire saw?
Asclepius and Hippocrates
N all the universe's cruelties
I guess I was blessed
It was only ever in the mix...
Of it all

* William Faulkner, *Requiem for a Nun,* 1951

K&V Nydam   somewhere near Sharon Qld.   Nov 2019

THE LUCKY ONES

Something stirred
Kin to catholic dreams
Aeon's bailing bond
For naught is as it seems

✳

Vintage thoughts
As minds do prowl
Palms connected
Joining souls and Tao

✳

Like ewers are
Where water's tamed
Writing's fine lines
Shaped obedient signs
Where hope 's contained

✳

We're force-fed duck
Just scribes do fuss
Awaiting blue-funk luck
To make foie gras of us

✳

Retorting to
Our heartfelt bay
The haughty ones
Royals for a day

✳

We're all made
On a potter's wheel
With that degree of effort
Surely, we mean something
To someone

✳

Take me, I'm yours
Cause we are... the lucky ones

Luck

Buffy Saint-Marie, 'It's My Way' – inspirational chord progression, springboard into something of
a call to arms-celebration-medium to high energy level musical piece.

Budapest – Amsterdam   2018

INNER CHILD and OTHER FAIRY TALES

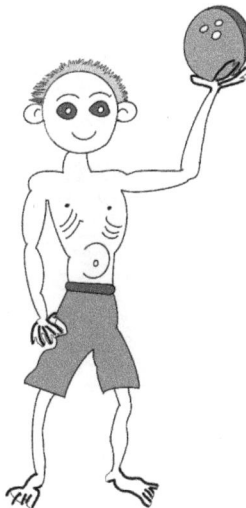

Coconut & Me

AND MY POINT IS

So – the truth of the matter is... at the end of the day
It – is what it is you know... moving forward – kind-a-like

Well – with all due respect... I will not lie
At – this point in time, some might say... It is what it is – whatever

You – only live once yeah... can I say – totes
Personally – I'm just saying, in terms of this and that

It – goes without saying, needless to say
Durr – shee' I think... know what I mean?

To – be honest, first and foremost... it goes without saying
Needless to say, Blah blah... woof-woof... I think

W$#@

BABUSHKA DOLL-8

Shed bling for a bit
On this want retreat
Dress-ups could stifle
May shackle your feet
An' have you dancing
To a shabbier drum
Or will it

The rout was called
By Babushka Doll-8
Forsake pretense
Remove the weight
The tenor was childlike
Be daffy – have fun
Run-run-run

Respite is sham to me
Ain't nothing I wanna flee
Whether plugged or unplugged
"Doesn't mean shit to a tree"

Casting off all guise
Makes it lighter to run
Time to advance
Back to when I was sure
Wondrous and wacky
Was the tactic du jour
Or was it?

Respite is sham to me
Ain't nothing I wanna flee
Whether plugged or unplugged
"Doesn't mean shit to a tree"

Cue all thirteen Dolls
Bid each one Thy name
Where there are no rules
None will be broken

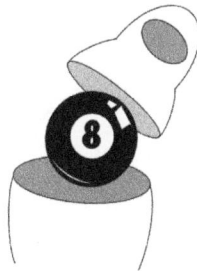

The 8-Ball

Bargara   Dec 2016

BEA SAVANT

Bea savant
Her heart
Her breath
Her latent load
All dialled down

✱

Senses tuned
To the timbre
Resonating
From the belly
Of the target zone

✱

Bea's buttons
Were ready tinder
She heard a hiss
Cracked its status
And was gone

Vanishing
Turning black
Bea dissolved
Melting amid
A flanker haze

✱

Next time
Bea will win
The grain of rice
Put there within
She can be proud
As a mouse
Inside a violin

✱

▼

K&V Nydam   Sydney-2-Madrid   June 2019

94

VOODOO MIRROR

Brea at three, sees a Queen
At five, it's Cinderella
At eight, she bawls because Brea
Finds an Ugly Sister
Then at twelve, Brea gets smashed
And breaks the voodooed mirror

You can't do everything
But you can do something
Sometimes a little-o-something real
Better than lots-o-nothing

Finn at four, finds an exit door
In his wardrobe mirror
At six, he does skits
Slapstick with his doppelgänger
At nine he finds, No is Yes
At fifteen finds Brea
Now there's a work in progress

You can't do much
When you sense you're at war
So ask yourself the question
What do you stand for?

At seventeen they're lovers
All be it sophomore
They look towards each other
Don't need mirrors anymore

Reference: *Poems & Laughter from the Purple Hat Ladies Tea Society*
The Purple Hat (Beautiful Women)

Bargara   June 2018

HELICOPTER OVER

James was four years older
Jess his *Billy the Kid*
He helicoptered over
That's what big bros did

Together, they played cowboys
With shootouts in the park
The games were never over
Until it got real dark

At times, Jess had trouble
Converting thought to speech
James was no help at all
A quick fix far from reach

Life-ache was a consequence
Her deepest terror babbled
Outside, silence answered
Inside, she was troubled

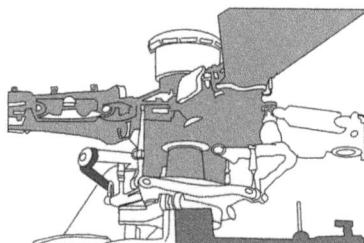

Chopper

Because of this; with no remiss
Jess built a shady role
She'd just stare; listen with care
To sweet-talk out the hole

When she spoke, words waited
Till Jess was eight drinks in
Her animus; her psyche base
Ever growing thin

And as she drank
She became less whole
An ogre preyed on a prancing foal
And Jess forgot, just how to feed her soul

What James felt, amped his life-ache
Her heart a phantom limb
When the shield was broken
His grit to fight eluded him

Where is her gist for feeling now
Where is her warm breath
Her gravitas bent time and space
Why – her ill-timed death

So, James, what do you do now
By night, lone in the park
The games were almost over
Until it got real dark

K&V Nydam   Shanghai/Bargara   July 2018

MEDICINE and SICK-OLOGY

Snappy Cat

DEAL WITH IT

Guess what... you're much more
Than a fine-edged tool
There's a phantom @ the wheel
And [s]he's driving you
(driving you... driving you)

Déformation professionnelle
A distortion-o-humanité
On a spectrum... and @ one end
You got it... be psychotic
(neurotic... robotic)

Magic thinking... when your brain
Wills to linking fake domains
N' fashion-o-passion... turns your purple patch pink
Where there's no refutation... you ort 'a rethink
(Purple... pink???)

The membrane between... life n' me
Is guarded by... a raw comedy
That's far too thin
Partnered with... a deeper fear within
(Deep... within)

There's an intersect... in almost everything
A sweet-spot... 4-ever moving
You can chase it but... you'll never win
Never win... never win
(Never win... never win)

When A Crystal Gaze Won't Cut It

So, what about pace... what about drift
What about grip-spin... what about shift
You transformed, optimised and grew me
Now here I am... you Deal with It

Short, sharp and snappy
We'll all do our best
To get to where... the goalpost
Will move to next
(Non-stop moving n' grooving)

What have... you done
Where... has it led
What... have you won
I was just having fun
(fun... 101)

All thing's... in life are hard
At times... a sideways advance
Is best for things... you just can't face
And you'll see more... @ second glance
(meanwhile dance... just dance)

So, what are you here for?
And what comes next
Why here at all
I'm a wee perplexed
(But I'll deal with it... deal with it)

K&V Nydam   Victoria Park Golf Club, Brisbane   Nov 2019

DOCTOR

I am a doctor – whatever that may mean
I do respond – to things that I have seen
and what I've seen – is more than a lot
that can't be unseen – or undone or forgot
I am a doctor

+

I am honoured – to walk 'long-side
have many thanks – and with grace abide
I've been taught 'n – I've been told
I'm thusly obliged – for behold
I... am a doctor

+

I have been wrong – more than twice
I have delivered – wretched advice
I'm not perfect – nowhere near
at times my best – will end in tears
Still, I am a doctor

+

Male Me a Doctor Forged by Fire

Nightfall comes – as it does
my mazy memory – jigsaws appear
not surge protected – from stabs of fear
they're needle-edges – but the crux is
I am *a doctor*

✚

I am a doctor – whatever that may portend
first responder – to the damage EMS send
the mental scars – how they wreaked
bedevilled voices – loudly creaked
I *am* a doctor

✚

All said and done – was it worth the price?
Roger that – I would pay twice
as "fire tests gold" – trauma tests the bold
in the end – I am told
I am *the doctor*

'Fire tests gold and adversity tests the brave' - Seneca

Bargara   Nov 2018

DOGS

Slat plastic doors
keep flap-flap-flapping
as the trolley wheels us
down another corridor
Wet black dogs
keep bark-bark-barking
reminding us
of the scars of war

Brain cells
keep spark-spark-sparking
beats-a-scatter
and signals poor
Drugs
are wearing thin-thin-thin
as real begins
to kick back in

Those dogs don't
come around here no more
Those dogs don't
come around here no more

Head still
keeps dump-dump-dumping
something's weird
yet at the verge
Our dogs
keep bark-bark-barking
"it shouldn't be like this
no more"

For God's sake
wake-wake wake-up
for our sake
maybe not

Those dogs don't
come around here no more
Those dogs don't
come around here no more

Dogs – Abbey Nydam

neurosurgical ICU, PHH, Little Bay, SYDNEY   1978

FAITH & PREJUDICE

Recall bars current time
Reprimanding bids to see
Real's a place for the unknown face
Faith is real
But treacherous to me

Peeling back onion skin
From out to in, fat to thin
Can you imagine rushing about?
Flaying them
From the inside out

Deconstruction catalyses
Understanding without doubt
Making purpose
Fantasise
A day without memory

Memory bans deft pasting
Never be particular
Be careful now, don't be too cool
When retrofitted
Memory's a fool

Retro fitting cause, leads to framing perversion
What others think about you, is not your business

Bargara   Feb 2019

FIRE ONLINE

My inner compass is swirling
My self-help plan is failing
F' my symptoms of stress
My backup is useless
Cause it's entirely online
I like, that I have your full attention

Who by Fire was a copout
Totally taken from Genesis
So now how can I trust
Who's the genius
An' who's also liable
I like, that I have your full attention

My bud Leonard Cohen
Alive till he died
Was so fond of showin'
His hunger for a story
Writ in a lyric... a poem
No less... counterfeit his line
I like, that I have your full attention

What was the source
Of his furnace of creation?
Who lights it?
And who extinguishes it?
And who really cares
It's all online, an' that's fine
I like, that I have your full attention

It's about re-counting
For the peeps online
It's about retelling, an' that's fine

Who is the source
Of this great fire of creation
So, tell me... who lights it?
And finally, who blows it out
I like, that I have your full attention

L Cohen 'Who By Fire'

Evas Way, Bargara   Nov 2019

HIGH

Tell me all about yourself
And of the unfortunate circumstance you bear
The thoughts that surround you
Are there to remind you
But you long to be free
From the troubles that they fear
Is it easy to be high
or are you just swimming... Mmmmm

You're overwhelmed and beside yourself
You look to the face of a friend to be kind
The thoughts that surround you
Are trying to drown you
So, you long to be free
From the troubles in your mind
Is it easy to be high
or are you just swimming
Are you feeling high and dry
or are you still swimming... Mmmmm

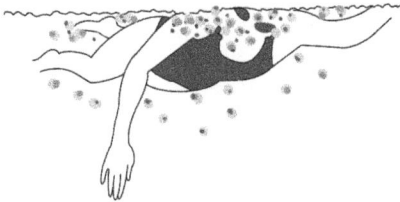

Easy 2B High

Menangle to Bargara   1988-2019

LES SAID

Les said
Hands off The Honey Jar
Do THAT
And you'll go far

Les said
Dial your WANTS to less
For calm
Dodge the lure of XS

Les said
Keep it simple and pure
Less fuss
More CONTENT F'sure

Les said
Stay the course, don't stray
Keep HEART
Wander and you'll pay

Les said
Fly below the radar
His GUARD Dropped
Mad monkeys ran amuck – LES DEAD RIP

In Loving Memory of a Night Gardener

Barcelona   Nov 2016

PARSIMONY'S SISTER

Parsimony's sister
Stole away our words
Binding us closer
When we sheathed our swords

We said more in silence
By quiet chaperone
Our bodies bickered louder
Fanning their own maelstrom

Drifting clear of sentences
About the jailers' misplaced key
Eyes penetrating eyes
We saw a safer place to be

Parsimony's sister
Sure had our six
Her superpowers were
Conversation's other tricks

Vox language was luggage
We had other use for lips
And there were other nuanced primal sounds
With our bodies sharing scripts

K&V Nydam   Santander, Spain   June 2019

PATANGA

Che casino
Who's in charge
Where's the boss-a-this...
Near wreck@large
The masses are fearful
My peeps feel the strain
Ten minutes from midnight
And probably pain

Our auras vibrate
Ahead of the junction
Blurred frescoes sign fate
Asking "what's our function"
Maybe consider
This cosmic jest
A morality play
A bona fide kicker

Dead ahead is Patanga
Depraved and sad
Where soul-matter fold
And folks go mad
You're likely to burn
On this midnight sojourn

Do be amazed
At what lies within
Two minutes from midnight
When the fun will begin
There in the mélange
Lights flash; lips babble
Speak now or hold tongue
Cause here comes trouble

Was it all done in vain
To get to this station
Was it stolid curt gruff
Heartbeat from elation
We are in charge
That could cost a lot
Nudging the throttle
Towards the sweet spot

Don't lay your trust
When your soul's on fire
In a two-finger salute
When straits are dire
Raise your fright
As a matter of course
Swerve and pull out
Seconds from midnight

Dead ahead is Patanga
Depraved and sad
Where soul-matter folds
And folks go mad
You're likely to burn
On this midnight sojourn

Patanga; 1800's Texas rancher term for when one over stimulates their aura so much that it ends up causing the etheric oscillations to collapse into an astral vortex, thus sucking all your energy reserves into a negative state of ionic sub-matter – Trace Bundy

K&V Nydam   Singapore   Jan 2019

111

RATTLESNAKE

The viper feigned, resetting poise
Hoax pantomiming sound-a-like
Should I be lured by the noise
And blind to the venom strike

Far from any mothers' smile
Dead ringer to a tympan's chatter
The issue is: How do you court
Those risky things, that do so matter

We were young, we were fragile
Our truths were thus concrete
We contorted and were agile
And danger smelt so sweet
A bite too bleak to call
Would that stop the dance
Life's metaphor: the tango
Where all is left to chance

Bare counterfeit or fair alarm
The bluster chosen by the wise
The favoured bliss that only comes
At moments when you improvise
Guile strikes with a bite
Black and white turn grey
You were right to stay outta
The rattlesnake's way

A bite too bleak to call, though
Would that stop the dance
Life's metaphor: the tango
Where all is left to chance
With riled head, eyeing all
Rising to a fearsome stance
She piqued a flight inside of me
Now all is left to chance

But if not for this
I'd not exist...

RS – Charley Boving

'Be we man, we are but dancers' – Killers

Bargara   2019

112

SAINT JUDE

I'm not the patron saint of lost and hopeless causes
I'm not responsible for how and why you got here
I'll do my best to help you kill the weeds that came from seeds you've sowed
Any more than that and you're on your own

'Cos I'm not here to be your private punching bag, no-no
The chaos that you wrought, you brought; it wasn't mine
I'll do my best to help but beyond that you own your actions
If that don't work, contact the one who made your mind

Hay Dude, my names not Jude
Hey Dude, I ain't Saint Jude
I'm only me...   [So, Go F#@k off]

I made my mind, despite due diligence and care
Like you, I have at times tripped on a phantom stair
So take some ownership, I don't mean to be unkind
'Cos it was you who got your thinking there

I'm gonna go and get some care in ways that I'll reciprocate
No, I won't punch or bite – or scrap and yell – or bait
I'm not the patron saint of lost and hopeless causes
And I hope for you, it's not too late.

K&V Nydam   August 2020   Bargara

SHERLOCK & DUMBO
[COME WALK WITH ME]

Imagine riding high
A mahout – reins in hand
While Dumbo's smirk hints
That he's in command

◆

Sherlock-hout and Dumbo
Play an innocent melee
Trading mind-f**k doubletalk
And loving each new day

◆

There's conflict cause the rider
Believes his life is art
Calling mutiny over
His massive mammoth's heart

◆

Come walk with me
As we cross the savannah
Walk wild with me
And feel it's windswept wonder
For it's the path of gold
At least that's what I've been told

◆

Elephant Man – Abbey Nydam

114

No-shit Sherlock
You an' all your knowledge
Please go forth and forage
But *don't* do so on your own

✦

Understand that solo
The tiger's swipe might get ya
Dark hell-loops, they'll scoop you up
To maul and then dissect ya

✦

And you – dearest Dumbo
You're pure and raw emotion
You trample through, your logic thin
With primal locomotion

✦

Sherlock – I need your foresight
Dumbo – I want your power
When 'Bo flaps his ears for flight
Sherl' shepherds from the
watchtower

✦

Come walk with me
We'll tour the savannah
Walkabout with me
And take-in all its wonder
For it's the path of gold
At least that's what I've been told

Jonathan Haidt introduces the **Elephant** and the **Rider** metaphor. ... But to us, the duo's tension is captured best by an analogy used by University of Virginia psychologist, Jonathan Haidt in his wonderful book *The Happiness Hypothesis*. Haidt says that our emotional side is the **Elephant** and our rational side is the **rider**.

K&V Nydam   Brisbane - Bundaberg   March 2020

SWEET REVENANT

We are stained // cause we abstained
To change for change is painful
We awoke // and sat up smiling
Whimsy-faced fenced by friends

Did it work for you? // we all asked
As though life's a drug-drawn vision
What a trip // we all had
Though kinda odd don't ya think

In a circle // with friends we asked
How do we change when change is painful?
Maybe pain // should be reframed
As breaking out or blossoming

Like a butterfly // or chrysanthemum
From a chrysalis and a bud
In a circle // with friends we passed
Questions round the room

Sweet Revenant // ennobled by assent
Bow now and re-join the circle
Like a butterfly // or chrysanthemum
From a chrysalis and a bud

We awoke // and sat up smiling
Whimsy-faced fenced by friends
What a trip // we all had
Though kinda odd don't ya think

TEMPORARY FRIEND

Pshaw... maw chagrin
I front your ghost again
Maybe not so curious
I'd hoped you'd done with that

So... we chanced to meet
A meek passing in the street
Pressed to masquerade
Life its own charade
Hearing a voice I knew
Now coming from a stranger

"Heading straight" proved cruel
The boredom became merciless
Your eyes... once mesmerised
Were gutted by the burden

Reality ever the stranger
Truth too lousy, you said
I saw fantasy drew you back
Promising refuge from your head

Ten years ago, you may have won
I'd hope to build ya confidence
Then pushback came
You'd bunt me counterarguments
We both know that arguments sting
With the scraps and melees they bring

So, you strayed from my arms
To some place god-forsaken
But you were already alone
Your soul was long ago taken
Forever lost at sea
Absent though in some way free
Denied her birthright to sing...
Charon hauled Chantel away
Denied her birthright to sing...
Life its own charade

Senseless Combat

Sydney   December 2017

WINDOW Mc GHOUL

window mc ghoul
cynic's euphemistic fool
see you play it cool in high stead
feel so tall...   that with no effort at all
you can topple any wall
'cept the callow dungeon pit of your head

macabre mannequin
don't mind you stepping in
to play its plastic puppet plague on fallowed minds
and forfeiture of soul's
the freeways only toll, to cross that bridge turn left
and spew your gutted brain

da-da-da dada

hey but I'm no god frog
stark on mushroomed log
to croak "the only good blessed thing's the turgid toad"
oh no-no
for quin mc ghoul, he's hooked
bent on a methedrine pool
he'll head or he'll behead you
he'll ruin, or he'll rule you
and I've heard it said, euphemists call cynics the fool

Coogee, Sydney   1972

118

ZEN [MADE FRIENDS WITH FEAR]

Time arrived
And found us up against the wall
All other options lost
We understood our hunch had hurt us

We made friends with fear
And slowly over cups of tea
Caught the dogmas faint reprise
'N came to understand its purpose

Fear's a mere traffic light
An amber-strobe warning
Go on with care, no true adieu
There is no cautious stalling

Ships are safe at harbour
But that's not why their builders labour
Despite what danger's flaunting
Real is always daunting

Sometimes the best way out is simply through
Howling "NO" to the universe
Only leaves you powerless; if anything, it causes pain
So just say "YES"

Sometimes the best way out is always through
Howling "NO" to the universe
Only leaves us powerless
@ a certain point, call on Zen...   Amen

'you can't start the next chapter of your life if you keep reading the last one'

K&V Nydam   Bargara   June, 2018

MORALITY, STRUGGLE and CONFLICT

Neilsen Park

A STREET OF 50 DOGS

Grace had been blessed
Hers had been a charmed life
Never vexed, nor distressed
Or ever known strife
Her proudest moment
Was her Graduation
Then in the wake became a mess

Getting pissed on she was...
Like the only fire hydrant
On a street of... 50 dogs

Grace tumbled out of place
Ejected from the catalogue
In our digital realm
She was raw analogue

Getting pissed on she was...
Like the only fire hydrant
On a street of... 50 dogs

Grace felt kinda thirsty
Her fuel gauge flickered low
In our carbon neutral world
She had fossil fuel in tow
Working in a M*A*S*H*
Resuscitating the dead
She failed to see the pointlessness
For a man with only half a head

Getting pissed on she was...
Like the only fire hydrant
On a street of... 50 dogs
Grace shutdown
So, she wouldn't weep
Stared at the ceiling
Before going to sleep
Grace idled, at a rest stop
On a drawn-out road

Still getting pissed on she was...
Like the only fire hydrant
On a street of...50 dogs

We all come with a story
A guarded reflection of our own journey
Luckily, we can choose which way to be drawn
T' wards the hydrant or the only patch of lawn
Either way, do your best
Not to get pissed or shat on
Here, on a street of... 50 dogs

Sniff

'Man is condemned to be free; because once thrown into the world, he is responsible for everything he does'
– Jean-Paul Sartre (1905–1980)

K&V Nydam   Bargara   February 2020

ANARCHIST

I wanna laugh and cry at the same time
I wanna nail the two-hour lunch
I wanna vindicate the long game
To authenticate my hunch

I need a Pablo and a Salvador
To raise me to total awe
Or bare a misconception
About the irony of war

With Franco on the case
Was chaos even at all a choice
With his white knuckles firm at the helm
Our hair did too turn white

His doctrine of progress
Would ne'er truly paralyse
The calamity that Franco brought
To the civil freeze, fight or flight

What do we do
When the dock line's gone
Caste adrift on a far-off sea
And I got a soldier here
Who won't stand down
He just won't let me be

I wanna face the masters
I wanna find that privileged place
Where real and divine coalesce
That Dali called paradise

I need a Pablo and a Salvador
To bring me to total awe
Maybe bare a misconception
About the irony of war

I wanna laugh and cry at the same time
I wanna to nail the two-hour lunch
To vindicate the long game
To authenticate my hunch

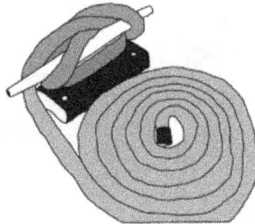

Dock (Mooring) Line

Socratic irony = Columbo's ploy
———————————
Madrid   June 2019

ARCHON'S HAND

I cut my Son – with Satan's rage
Felt like justice – I must own
That done – my hand was paralysed
Feelings numb – bare to the bone

I said – the Beast I would become
Was a hunted – haunted soul
That said – that so and so's last wish
Was this – so listen... then extol

I tried so hard – to justify
And clarify – I did my best
Slow to the wisdom – Abel gained
Said Archon – but who would have guessed

◆

Matters intersect and collide
Melee to you – mandate to me
All serious – maybe so
So, listen...

◆

Cain asked "Father," when I was done,
"Would you bid me to forgive you?"
I said "Yes" – Eve said "No"
Oozing eloquence – brut-brilliant coup

Birthright – Bloodlines
Seduction times – do you forgive me
Genesis – Muddle pasts
Betraying times – could you forgive me?

◆

I cut my Son – with Satan's rage
Felt like justice – I must own
That done – my hand was paralysed
Feelings numb – bare to the bone

Archon

Reference: Leonard Michaels, *Eating Out*

K&V Nydam   Bargara/Shanghai   May 2018

ARMS RACE

[Asus2]
It's just an arms race
Foreign cadres seek to interfere
So, take a broad view
Not much changes year to year [to year]

[Dsus6/Bm7/G/A]
Segue to you
On chiffon wings
Your key morass
The genius of things

Misinformation
Spread from there to here
Keeps getting better
No coward's tryst without a tear

Grilled and trampled
Awkward moments forever shared
Softball questions
Never answered, no one dared

Segue to you
On gossamer wings
Your key morass
The genius of things

Dark suited ladies
Talk in tongues that do not lie
Opposing tones that forever
Flash and hypnotise

Rash and quixotic
Dumb yet poetic, as befits the sleuth
Dare, go get it if you want it
That single point of truth

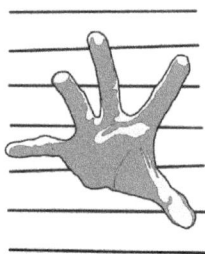

Hands Need Arms

Dubai   2018

BLOOD RED ROSE [LION]

Who... said run
Who bade the Sun... rise
Vowing light... sown to see
And rain... to cool the horses

Waging war by course-o-night
With semantic night-vis bows
Till the morn... saw it bright
Blood Shot Red Rose
Yet most of all our nerves bled
Editing each-every word we said

Now it's fine
No much better than that
Said it's fine
No much better than that
It's OK
No even better than that
It's YEAH
Even better than that

Remember me as the sound of
laughter
Hemi-legionnaire... demi-clown
A *Fool on the Hill*... mind never still
Loath to see... or ever frown
Yet most of all our nerves bled
Editing each word, we said

Now it's fine
No much better than that...

Who... said the fighter
Jester... two-faced mutineer
Who would oppose a mere
songwriter
Blood Shot Red Rose

Legionnaire's Light

Was a violent dawn; us an oafish babble
Flouting odds a woeful loss befell; them too easily tricked into battle

Coogee Bargara   1972-2018

BOY EATS FIRE

Outside da space, were verity bites
'N' friends ask "whatcha doin'?"
Outside the play, were real fires burn
What cause, 'R' you pursuin'?

Outside da box, where "true" resides
And talk's made easier by wine
Mise en scène sits, like nothing's lost
Cause all's fine, read the sign

Relentless-n-fixated
Not to be placated
BOY casts a line, into d-abyss
His voice for now vacated
After all, BOY was just putting out fires
After all, he was just putting out fires
After all, BOY was just putting out fires
After all, he was just putting out fires

Pressure points, point to where
Nerves are raw @ bottlenecks
Emotions drive without a doubt
Be sure, it's deep-n-complex

This crazy mix has been workin'
On normal for a while
Kept cool under wraps, with watermelon caps
Head's shaded as love is traded

I'll buy envy
From those who can spare
Botchin' scorn with inattention
Please do be aware
The skies not contained
This boy's rules define
Yet still not fit for purpose
T'was not what he had in mind

Yet still not fit for purpose
Who'd say BOY ran in vain
Was it his soul that simply missed
What he would not deign
After all, he was just putting out fires
After all, he was just putting out fires
After all, he was just putting out fires
After all, he was just...

Buggara   March 2019

DIDI

Halfpenny Hitler's
Big sister's a killer
When Di made us laugh
We shattered like glass

Gripped by the riot
Bit head-swell pathetic
We found ourselves pitted
Mid-goal, mid-aesthetic

Halfpenny Hitler's
Sister's full quid
Didi did bad
At all that she did

Her half-witted brother
Did never compare
T' Di wreaking havoc
All beware

Him a mere seraph
To Di's lightning rod
Her greed for power
Was her need to be God

So ultra contraire
Dependant on view
Context, mindset
Provenance too

Di's take-off point
Was Dame Nature
Those able, survive
All others fall

Di did assemble
A random array
Mute odds and sods
Airs entertained

Rarely a woman
For time or fact
Didi recalled
Fake news with no tact

So why is it he
We evermore cite
And not his Big Sister
With all her might

The losers are pilloried
Marionettes for all times
While the Master Handlers
Are acquit of their crimes

Melbourne   Oct 2018

FAUST

His all-conceited claim
Matched his cocky core-belief
No worthless tiers of detail here
No more a drudger, now d' CHIEF

Urgent matters 4-all to note
Bounds pushed beyond d' pale
Undeserved entitlements
Does it matter that he failed?

We'll just have a good time
We'll all have a ball
Be impromptu, nothing's planned
A Grand Old Free-4-All

Discipline, who needs it
Permissiveness, its own reward
Goethe gave us carte blanche
"Your-bad", if you're bored

So, who asked Faust and why?
@ his first romantic vision
He was later strum und drang
'Till he understood d' schism

Depravity, perverse maybe
Stole d' wind from his sail
In the extreme, his rambling dream
Tread an uber tizzy trail

We'll just have a good time
We'll all have a ball
We'll take a bow to Goethe
And his Grand Old Free-4-All

Sealed with a Kiss

The Devil Made Me Do It

K&V Nydam   Brisbane-2-Singapore   Nov 2019

FLAG

Ground zero found our hero
Again, at peace with war
Battling over borders
Blurting Gatling gun-like orders

Defending someone else's soil
Yet – but for tyranny or destiny
He could 'a been so easily
Born on the other side

The flag fluttered an utterance
"I am a wind vein channelling tyrants'
Head-rush-tumbled-dry blood"
Trampolining in response
To whichever way the wind blows

Impish and impertinent
Watch the zipping missiles vent
Deafening ground zero and defining our hero
When and whenever he went
Directed by a nonchalant flag

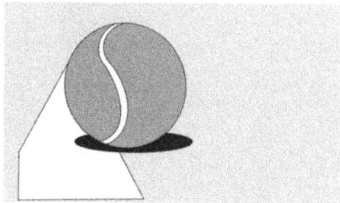

Lineball

Darwin NT   September 2020

HOUSE: PIAGET BEDLAM
[ONE STEP OFF REAL]

Go analyse, data for facts
Elucidate, fiction for truth
The bona fide portrait, of what is real
And what is the blaze of youth

In these rowdy times – bawdy stuff
We were all touched, with heart-felt zeal
A mad comedy, mayhem of sorts
You're at your best, one step off real

Seriously, don't take yourself too deep
Clearly, don't seek amends
Gravely, you'll end up in a place
The Cabaret House of Kid's Bedlam

It's a bit of a stretch from burlesque
But it meets the need to stay mortal
Life's a Cabaret House – of sorts
Entered via a foreign portal

Try dehumanising, what's that?
Life can be brutal, and that is what you'll feel
Tell the privileged kids, you're always at your best
One step off, one crazy step off... real

Kelly's Beach   September 2019

SATYR AND THE END-GAME

Stoned by sight-n-scent
As *all* was laid bare
Trumpets blew to validate
And all I could do was stare
At the Satyr on heat
Sure, and emotion-immune
Running down Lothario's deal
Scored by Natura's tune

High-five to the mother load
And cue our carnal concerns
For urgent lust is dangerous
But will we ever learn?
Lust it just don't nurture
Lust does not remain
Lust retreats on fleeting feet
Back from whence it came

Teardrops they will come
When jeopardy is gone
Teardrops 'ill wash away
And so, cleanse everyone
No prep for the crevasse
No prenup for the menace
Teardrops will be absorbed
Absolving everyone

Writ by constellation
And guided by the stars
At the end of the day
We'll get to where we are
We'll write-up our memoirs
Pen the magic and banal
Windblown like Mariah
Bugle in the finale

Allowing for transmission
Satyr dazed along
He sure hell got the answer right
But the question was all wrong
Issues like "is life a sprint
Or more a marathon?"
Who gets to measure who you are?
And to where you belong?"

Do you seek out danger?
Are you energised by that?
A scalding bright white flame
Far from your habitat
Fiery coupling bares no shame
There's no wrong in the format
It's just a long way off
From the endgame

Satyr

K&V Nydam   Sydney   March 2020

VACANT EYE

He checked his weapon at the door
Grant's need to kill, right now suspended
Hell, what-a-day it's-been
Sure-glad, it was upended

Shay booked her conscience at the exit
Her work was work, it was begun
She dropped her wears there on the floor
Chasséd up, to fake her fun

Everyone wants to be in the Garden
Regarde-la the vacant eye
Everyone wants to live in Eden
Everyone wants to kiss the sky

They paused their converse on connection
A noise-graffiti, the score unwritten
The finger wag, at once forgotten
Both feigned a smile, faux-gladly bitten

Shay's soul was n'er Granted
That didn't matter any more
Grant's wish was kind-a similar
Both sat their demons down by the door

Everyone wants to be in the Garden
[We all check something – We all feign something]
Everyone wants to live in Eden
[We all feign something – We all check something]

Kane left his caring in the carpark
Surplus to needs, where he'd go
Concord – nothing but an anchor
Concern – a simple sideshow

Leah dropped her hope into the ocean
Clearly lighter now it's gone
A race to run – worlds to conquer
Kane had passed her his baton

They drew a line in the water
Accosted the waves and kept praying
Kane faced leeward to protect her
Leah was deadpan focused again

Vacant Eyes

K&V&A Nydam   Bargara   Spring 2018

WHAT THE ...

Where were you, when I needed you
Where were you, My Dear
You who call yourself God
Ha! You're nowhere near

With your belly, full of Bacchus
I'm just your cheap sex toy
For you to wet your dumb wick in
You're just a Sad Little Boy

Soul Searching
Yelling and screaming
I laugh at you, My Dear
You want direction, to redemption
I wouldn't leave from here

Your help was underwhelming
I was affected by your trick
The disorder, was yours alone
You were all right dipstick

"We got your back" you said
Grand words gone up in smoke
My trust, was well betrayed
You My Dear, are just a joke... What the...

Who is, the Child here?
Who is, the My Dear?
Who's the Doe, and who's the Buck
And who really even gives a... What The...

Windmill Café, Bargara   August 2019

WIZARD MAN

Something strange, Mr. Dore
Maybe scandal, tell us more
Make a Beeline for the draw
We could get a taste for it

For those few certain to
Recognise the politic
Jericho and who else knew
Odd thing, our shtick

Do the maths, turn the wheel
Foreign fair, this Faustian deal
This tack is fancy, cop a feel
An hour's ride from Brunswick

Don't set-forget, have QA done
No matter where it'll takes us
We will never waver

Chant and rhythm, do collide
Notes and time, tantamount
For the rest, a seat ringside
In the shielded cockpit

Held myths are more valuable
Prized and safe in a madman's pocket
A bit of ballast, purely practical
Piquing harmony, like a prophet
Let go, uh-oh, oh-no
Wizard Man

'Euphemism is a euphemism for lying'
– Bobbie Gentry, singer and songwriter (b. 27 Jul 1944)

Bundaberg   Jan 2018

MORTALITY and IMMORTALITY

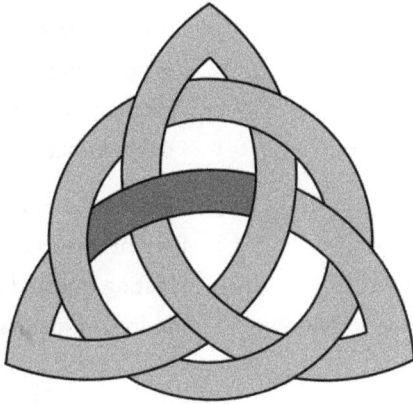

I AM MAN

Imposter Syndrome struck
Had me a sitting duck
After far too many years
Riding luck for my good fortune

Imposter Syndrome bashed me
Found me wounded, weak and lean
But too few days thereafter
I felt the best I'd ever been

Then another syndrome mauled me
Was I malingerer or fighter
So, I switched myself to grateful
On a grayscale getting lighter

Now my ache 's converted to
A glooming decrescendo
An Irrelevancy Syndrome
My looming junkyard innuendo

I wonder what comes next
What result is yet to follow
For these diagnostic boxes
God only knows they ring so hollow

Where is the humanity
Where is my warming hug
Wherever is the honest smile
Beyond the cold hard drug

Neurotic, that sure sounds like me
I maraud that territory
For my vast subconscious dreads
Lurk in a deep and dark quarry

There are layers upon layers
Like an onion skin travelling in
Through small and ever smaller orbits
My nano-space capsule fighting tailspin

Imposter syndrome. Duck!
I'm sorry but I'm no damn God
After far too many years
I declare that I'm verily flawed

I am man... I am vulnerable
I'm flotsam and shipwrecked
Floating free and anchorless
No longer needing to be perfect.

Ref: Helen Reddy, 'I Am Woman'

K&V Nydam   Bargara   August 2020

RI PETE

Pete was dark
Curious
Decadent
And in too deep
Driven
Devoid direction
'Cept chucking fear aside
As befit a soiled perspective

Lone wolf
Bone wanton
Born in autumn
Short a spring and summer
Covert – forgone
Exploring what heat was left
Dodging the ice within

Life
Took hold
Pulled him under
And then deeper
Groaning
A thought
Blind luck
And happenstance

Seeking the Honey Pot
He never trusted
Missing the Sweet Spot
Misdirected
Pete never rusted
Passing on
His body perfect

Dangerous and
Odourless
Too much alive
To change his mind
Pete got
What others could not
RI Pete

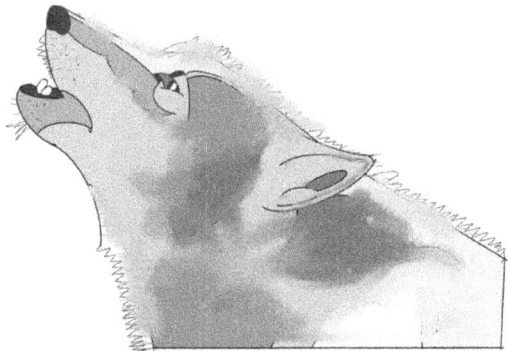

RIP

Bargara   2018

REGARDEZ LES ÉTOILES
[LOOK TO THE STARS]

Take in the night
Fine dine with care
Raise your glass
To all that's up there

Unseal your eyes
Jimmy your heart
Let *son et lumière*
Parade its part

★

The night's scaffold ignites
Amidst the galaxy's blaze
And with your Pilgrim's clay feet
You'll gate-crash a new phase

★

The nightscape's empyreal
With its shimmering luminance
Ancient melodies will trumpet
And you will hear them blare

★

We woman and man
When we fell on stage
A sole flash in the pan
Until coming of age

★

Us coy support folk
Cue crickets and clappers
Don't assume your life matters
In our troupe of tawdry slappers

We sought peace on Earth
So, we made war on Mars
Only to learn
Don't mess with the stars

★

We're nothing but a clump
Of carbon-based nanobots
Our rank in the bigger scheme
Is conflated by idiots

★

Fasten your eyes
To each solar flare
Your umbra will shudder
And junk Vanity Fair

★

You wanna know who you are?
The truth is stark
With no stars overnight
We'd be in the dark

★

Go heed the night
With you mind ajar
Don't be snared on the gnarl
Raise your gaze, open your heart
Regardez les étoiles

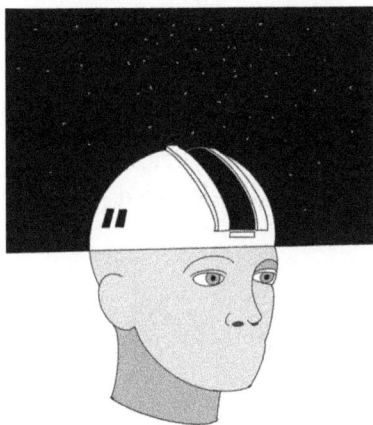

Observatory Man

K&V Nydam   Bargara   April 2020

THE WEIGHT #2

Hi-ya – what's up?
I hear your hush clarion
so, what are you now?
white noise or contrarian

By your raison d'être
and I'd say by design
you are less mighty now
mere *passé* foe of mine

From here on out
I don't cue when you roar
don't incite nor fashion me
make an ache I abhor

Your mire duped me once
insist I trudge a path
your weight a yoke to hinder
my ambition and advance
in Nazareth shone
Gabriel's star
try play me now
bet you don't get far

Who owns whom
That's the question
the player or the monkey
what's your suggestion?

Angels fly
for they revel in lite
buck THE WEIGHT
and discover their flight

Mad Bad Monkey

'Angels can fly because they take themselves lightly'
– G. K. Chesterton, *Orthodoxy* (1908), Chapter VII: The Eternal Revolution

Bargara   2018

146

VALKYRIES CRY

IMMORTALS watch, as VALKYRIES cry
For a sleep, that ne'er arrives
Think-a-days, without a night
For THEM, that's what it's like

Afore DAWN, descends a HUSH
Before sunrise, upsets the quiet
Breathing starts, beating a RUSH
Birthing MAN, day-born-o-night

Blasé GODS, BE wholly sure
Dat cowered MORTALS, e'er want more
Take what's given, let else fly
Grab the "NOW", lose the "WHY"

Brother SOMEONE, taught me something
Called it faith, atop-o-nothing
Crazy GODS, with bare-skinned women
Better flesh, ne'er been written

From a MILLION, stories spoken
Treasured lessons, tenets told
Placed a limit, on our reign
Just once, no "TRY AGAIN"

When GIANTS fight, MORTALS hurt
Treading dark and deadly waters
The bonus is the SOULS plenty
Fleeting LIFE, hogs the SPOTLIGHT

The doing's NOW, the END's da-prize
While DEITIES wait, VALKYRIES cry
For an end, that ne'er arrives
Imagine days, that have no night
For THAT, is WHAT it's like

When Choosing the Slain, Valkyries Cry

Everyday living is what does us in; only death gives life meaning

Bargara   Feb 2018

MY CHILDREN

Through others, we become ourselves.
– Lev Vygotsky, psychologist (17 Nov 1896–1934)

Three Gods

BAB – HOPE & WHOLE

Brain-State, State-a-Mind
Occupation, Tune-a-Soul
Mass connection, physical
All these things, make us whole

Contribution, to family
Art & craft, labour leisure
Best friends, playmates
Private growth, reshapes
Call it higher nature

Sure, I'd love to make you smile
Beam that face of academe
Don't run, you've ready won
True self-esteem, daughter-mine
You got it... now flaunt it

Daughter-mine, a minefield
My inadvertent muse
You'll [so soon] overtake me
But I don't mind,
Don't deal a lame excuse

Mental-state, State-o-Hope
Attitude-o-Soul, in the race
If you're not on the edge,
You're takin' up too much space

Bargara   Dec 2018

Dr. Bab

BEYOND THE DOME

What if we found the place
Where the horizon meets the sky —
If we finally found the answer
To a lifetime of asking why
What would we do, and upon which direction
Would we cast our soul's reflection
Could we cease our quest forever
Stop stalking revelations
And flee the firmament
To find home beyond the dome

They say the past is history
And what's beyond is a mystery
To live life in the moment
Is to end all the witchery
But how... do we live in the now
And build a home beyond the dome

What if we found a face
Where our lips meet with creation
If we finally found a soulmate
With whom to forge a new foundation
How would we do it, and from what new direction
Would we take in our newfound connection
Could we drop with the questions
And live in the now
At our novel home beyond the dome

Flammarion Engraving

In the end the past is done
But that don't stop us from having fun
To live life in the moment
Pull the witchery undone
But how... to live within the now
At our home beyond the dome

What if we found a place
Where we all could co-exist
If we peeled back a teeny space
Where sea and sky uphold a tryst
What on earth would we do
If we could easy crawl out through
To beyond where the heavens
Meet the deepest of deep blue
Would we then stop asking why
And press on in the now
Peering in forevermore from outside the dome

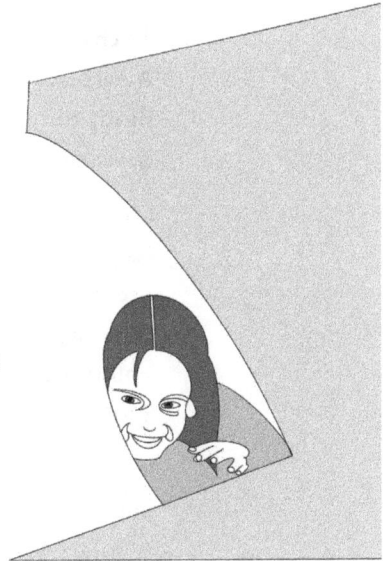

Flammarion Engraving Take #2

K&V Nydam   Bargara   Oct 2020

DARK HORSE

Where you at
Where you bin
And where you off to next
My dear dark horse
Sweet son-o-mine
Show to me your manifest

Hearing your harangue
I promptly sort
To charge steadfast your way
A bald-faced defender
Ready to counter
By listening to what you had to say

I shook my head
As you bled
I couldn't do a thing
Shielding my eyes
Half-turning away
Surrogate to your aching

It'll improve, I know it will
But pain is the bill you must pay
A bittersweet pill, my sympathies to you
As life's symphony pursuantly plays

My dark horse has broken loose
I no longer hold the reins
My dark horse is flying free
Traversing the open plains

K&V N   Kelly's Beach   June 2020

HOPSCOTCH

Usher me onward to my holy grotto home
Guide me 'long the path toward my lowly catacomb
Drain me 'til all my colour's gone
Bleach me sickly white as bone

Whisper sweetly to me so no one else can hear
Form a lattice 'round me no man can commandeer
Channel a talisman to protect our souls made mortal
With an axe to pick the frozen sea inside of us all

Mute the chatter ceaseless in thine mind
Stake a piece of quiet upon higher ground
Though the dirt be worth near naught if mined
The view up here is Heaven bound

Grab at and grasp the passing of time
Still it, validate it, before your toll bell chimes
Stalk the moment for you know you must
And to each cicada shell, mix a tincture of lunar dust

A reckoning is beckoning; something weird has awoken
The wingman calls compellingly, warnings have been spoken
The pavement's poorly lit, and suddenly you step on it
Crack goes your mother's back, and it cannot be unbroken

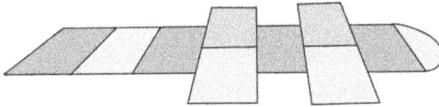

Reference: 'A book must be an axe for the frozen sea inside of us' – Franz Kafka, novelist (1883–1924)

K&V Nydam   Bargara   July 2020

DINNER WITH KATE

Sh' called me a hippie...
T' was exactly what I'd hoped she'd see
I little bit dipsy... maybe even trippy
My preferred vision of me... right here... right now... today

What garb do you grab... from your dress-up box
To set y' persona... an' who d' you wanna be
Eschewing the limelight... no leeway for stage freight
Hell, I *wanna* be this and here... today
I little bit dipsy... maybe even trippy
My preferred vision of me... hooray

I'll go home... and take the makeup off
Laugh out loud... in silence
And tomorrow assign... a different role
Playing my own stylist... right here... right now... today

So, who are you... after your audition?
Who do you dress as Kate?
What masquerade do you petition
For this, our dinner date?

Your haute couture... was for sure
What you hoped I'd see
High-end fashion... simple and pure
The tables turned on me... right here... right now... today

Kate's precision... to her vision
Tuned to what she wished to be
For our fashion tête-à-tête
Today... at my dinner with Kate

Dad's 60th Dessert

Kate Gould

FREE FROM THE HAMSTER WHEEL

I'd like a life that's free from the hamster wheel please
I wish to choose to want exactly what it is that I want
I aim to park my own meaning on the world and on myself
And set me in the driver's seat, unfettered and upfront

The two wheels in front will steer my purpose 'n direction
The two behind me will remain there – spinning on their spool
I hope to let all four wheels gain momentum – not perfection
And let my freewill guide me, with logic as my fuel

I'd like to think about progressing to really fix the problem please
Instead of thinking of the problem's pretence and presence itself
I'd love if each new day was not an echo of the former
I need my yesterdays stored out of reach, high on a shelf

Will I – won't I – with who and when?
Yep, I'm fixating 'bout dopamine again
This constant vigil has turned obsession
Will I ever learn life's intended lesson?
The old "wills or won't"s are all out of frame
Thoughts of old lovers are erased from the picture
Instead, I'd prefer love's pure and plain
Precocious and perky younger sister

I'd like intrusiveness of thought, justly trumped by curiosity
I'd like to share, to care for and connect within our universe
I'd like all parts of consciousness to live in splendid harmony
Being haunted by imagined loss is fraud and so perverse

I'd like my life to be free of the hamster wheel please

Hamster Wheel

"How you think about a problem is more important than the problem itself ..." – Norman Vincent Peale

K&V Nydam   Bargara   August 2020

HOW'S THAT

This wicket game must end
Just how an' when, will depend
On the play and the chances
That you take

●

Dumb shots, sure you've played 'm
Thank God, you've learnt some from 'm
You're like a cat with extra lives
'Else how on earth, did you survive

●

I don't know how
But we're still standing
On the right side
Of the dispatch box
I don't know how
Grateful by the grace
I'm still batting
Smashing balls

●

It's a jungle out there
Fielders prowling everywhere
But watch how they cower
To our fire and flair

●

We'll keep our spirits alight
Build suspense in the air
Breathe life into leather
And whack it anywhere
Grateful by the grace
Till our flames do expire
And we finally retire
To urn the ashes

■

Dispatch Box

K&V Nydam   Melaka-Singapore   2 Dec 2019

KEEPER

Dad, he's a keeper, she said
But I'm not ready to be kept
Not ready for that yet
What do I do?
Can I put him on ice?

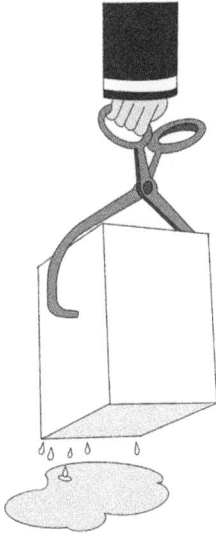

The Ice-Man Cometh

Brisbane   2014

[KEEP YA] PLANS IN THE SAND

What ya gunna do when you grow up
What you gunna 'chieve B' fore times up
What kinda mark will they leave
On ya tombstone

They told me "go to uni"
Chalk-up a paper, score a degree
Make a motza, earn a shitload
Then die

If it's the first 1,000 days that shape ya
Then why can't I understand
Why something so unrecalled
Is so "ultra-grand"
Keep your goals in concrete
And ya plans in the sand

So now here I am
Wit' shit loads-a-paper, what a scam
Imposter syndrome looms big, grown up
But I still don't know who I am

What ya gunna do when you grow up
That's quite a question
An' the answer is?
F**k the question

Reframe
Burn the page
N' never age
Be a dancer
Just don't grow up

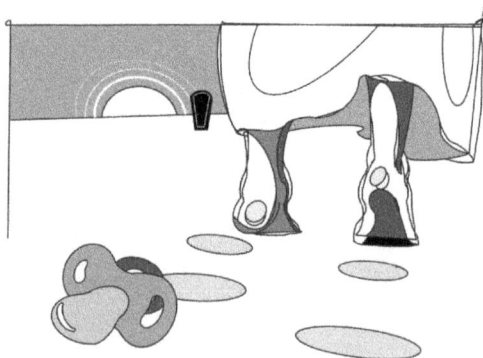

Keep Ya Plans and
Feet in the Sand

Bargara   Oct 2019

RIDE DAUGHTER RIDE

well I don't know that much about it
but I'm letting the matter go
seems there's nothing to do about it anyway
nothing good will ever come of it
so, I'm just letting the matter ride

for love, will you be gentle
and I'll give you myself a gift to the wind
ride daughter ride
I hope you don't miss it
for the ships are all coming in

people seem to like it
but never touching it when it is there
wishes to rapid, to hope you'll never be catching
you can't see your living in a forest mist
a mysterious haze

Let it Ride

Coogee, Sydney   1973

THE END